This We Believe

A Study Guide to the Teachings of Seventh-day Adventists

Erwin Gane & Leo Van Dolson

Pacific Press Publishing Association
Boise, Idaho
Oshawa, Ontario, Canada

Editorial Office
12501 Old Columbia Pike
Silver Spring, MD 20904

Principal Contributors
Erwin R. Gane
Leo R. Van Dolson

Associate Editor
Lyndelle Chiomenti

Assistant Editor
Charlotte Ishkanian

Pacific Press Coordinator
Jerry D. Thomas

Art and Design
Lars Justinen

Scripture references other than from the King James Version quoted by permission in this quarterly are as follows:

NASB. From The New American Standard Bible, copyright © The Lockman Foundation 1960, 1968, 1975. Used by permission.

NEB. From The New English Bible, copyright © by the Delegates of the Oxford University Press and the Syndics of the Cambridge University Press, 1961, 1970. Used by permission.

NIV. From the New International Version, copyright © 1978 by New York International Bible Society. Used by permission.

RSV. From the Revised Standard Version, copyright © 1946, 1952, 1971, 1973 by the Division of Christian Education of the National Council of the Churches of Christ in the USA, and used by permission.

NRSV. From the New Revised Standard Version of the Bible, copyright © 1989 by the Division of Christian Education of the National Council of the Churches of Christ in the USA. Used by permission. All rights reserved.

Contents

Meet the Writers of This Quarter's Lessons

Erwin R. Gane is the editor of the Adult Sabbath School lessons. While Dr. Gane has pastored several churches on two continents, most of his service has been in the field of education. He taught at Avondale College in his native Australia, and at Union College and Pacific Union College in the United States. He received his M.A., M.Div., and M.Th. degrees from Andrews University and a Ph.D. degree from the University of Nebraska. Dr. Gane and his wife, Winsome, have two grown sons.

Leo R. Van Dolson is a former editor of the Adult Sabbath School lessons. His career has included pastoral work in the U.S. and Japan, and teaching at Pacific Union College and the Loma Linda University School of Health. He holds a Ph.D. in educational administration from Claremont College. Dr. Van Dolson has served as an editor on *Ministry, Life and Health,* and the *Adventist Review*. He has authored or co-authored 18 books and has written several adult teachers' aids. He and his wife, Bobbie Jane, have two adult children.

Introduction

The Bible is the ultimate authoritative sourcebook of spiritual truth. It contains all the teachings necessary for our salvation. After incorporating the main focus and doctrines of Scripture in his Revelation, the apostle John concluded: "If any one adds to them, God will add to him the plagues described in this book" (Rev. 22:18, RSV). The point he makes is not that the Lord has not chosen and will not choose others to impart divinely revealed messages to the church and the world. Rather, it is that whatever inspired revelation comes after the writing of the last book of the Bible, it will not teach new doctrines. Every teaching essential for the salvation of mankind is contained in the Holy Scriptures of the Old and New Testaments.

The twenty-seven lessons presented in these two volumes represent an earnest, prayerful attempt to explain the Bible's leading doctrines. In February 1991, the delegates to the World Sabbath School Curriculum Committee, meeting at the General Conference of Seventh-day Adventists in Silver Spring, Maryland, voted to request the adult Sabbath School quarterly editors to prepare a series of Bible lessons that can be used for classes, seminars, and home Bible studies. The lessons that follow have been prepared in response to that request.

The authors of these lessons have kept in mind three main target audiences: (1) those who are not committed Christians but who wish to understand the fundamentals of the faith; (2) Christians who are seeking to broaden and deepen their knowledge of God's Word and their relationship with Jesus Christ; (3) those who wish to share their faith in response to Jesus' great commission to "make disciples of all nations" (Matt. 28:19, 20, RSV).

We urge those wishing to lead others in Bible studies to place the lessons and the companion volume, entitled *This We Believe*, volume 3, in their hands, allowing them to search the Scriptures for themselves. Then the instructor should meet with these interested persons, reviewing major points, answering questions, and applying the Bible teaching to life needs, interests, and challenges.

The lessons do not necessarily have to be studied in the order presented in this volume. Because individual needs and interests vary greatly, it is helpful to begin with those subjects and issues of greatest concern to the student. Neither must all of a lesson be presented in one session; part of one lesson may be sufficient at one time.

The prayer of the authors is that multitudes around the world will find in these lessons and the companion volume helpful tools for a clearer understanding of God's Word.

Lesson 14

Baptism

BAPTISM ATTESTS TO OUR UNION WITH CHRIST. One well-known preacher often says, "Sitting in a church house no more makes you a Christian than sitting in a henhouse makes you a chicken." Neither does baptism *make* us Christians. It should testify that the Holy Spirit is dwelling in us and has led us to repent of our sins and to desire to live a new life in Jesus.

Baptism "originated in pre-Christian times. It was practiced by the Jews as a means of receiving proselytes to Judaism. . . . It is significant that the Jewish leaders did not question John concerning the validity of the rite of baptism, but only his authority to administer it (see John 1:19-28). Baptism was also practiced by the Essenes in connection with their religious rites. In *Khirbet Qumran*, which was probably the center of the Essenes, several tanks with steps leading into them have been discovered. . . . These may have been used for baptismal rites, which apparently involved immersion."—*SDA Bible Dictionary*, p. 118. John's authority for administering baptism came directly from God. (See John 1:33.)

KEY THOUGHT: By baptism we confess our faith in the death and resurrection of Jesus Christ, and attest to our death to sin and our purpose to walk in newness of life.

"Know ye not, that so many of us as were baptized into Jesus Christ were baptized into his death? Therefore we are buried with him by baptism into death: that like as Christ was raised up from the dead by the glory of the Father, even so we also should walk in newness of life" (Rom. 6:3, 4).

WHAT BAPTISM IS.

What adaptation of the rite of baptism did John the Baptist make in order to help the people of his day identify with the work of cleansing necessary to prepare for the coming of Christ? Mark 1:4, 5.

Although there were Old Testament antecedents that John the Baptist would have known about—ritual washings and cleansings, and the story of Naaman—he taught that the rite would involve spiritual cleansing. Thus it was to be more than a mere ritual or physical cleansing. He asked the people to demonstrate by their baptism that they recognized their sinfulness and were repentant. John's call to baptism indicated that a drastic change was necessary to prepare people for Jesus' coming.

If baptism signifies a confession of sin, why was Jesus baptized? Matt. 3:15.

Acts 2:38 contains Peter's admonition to new converts to the Christian faith to be baptized as a symbol of the remission of sins. Having never sinned, Jesus did not need to be baptized as a symbol of confession for sin. By being baptized He identified Himself with the sinner, who needs God's righteousness. He set an example for those who desire to confess their sins and be united with Him.

What do we learn about the Christian practice of baptism from the instruction that Jesus gave in Matthew 28:18-20 and Mark 16:15, 16?

Baptism attests not only to our death to sin but also to our resurrection to a new life in Christ. (See Rom. 6:4, 5.) Baptism is to be performed in the name of the Father, Son, and Holy Spirit. It follows clear instruction in and willingness to practice all things Christ has commanded. The promise is given that Christ will be with those who make this commitment from that time on.

Jesus indicated that we are to be baptized not only by water but also by the Spirit. What does this experience have to do with my becoming a member of the body of Christ?

7

WHAT BAPTISM DOES.

It gives evidence that Christ is Lord of our lives. Ancient large baptisteries attest to the vital importance of baptism by immersion to the early church. The rite demonstrates to both the church and the world that we have died to sin and have been raised to new life in Christ. Paul writes: "For all of you who were baptized into Christ have clothed yourselves with Christ" (Gal. 3:27, NASB).

How is confession of faith in God and acceptance of Jesus as Lord of our lives tied into the rite of baptism? Rom. 10:9; Acts 16:30-34.

In addition to bringing Christians into a richer and closer relationship with God, baptism brings them into a new relationship with Christ's church on earth. Baptism publicly identifies us as Christians—members of the body of Christ. (See Acts 2:41, 47; Gal. 3:27-29.)

In a Voice of Prophecy radio sermon years ago entitled "The Golden Stairs to the Golden City," H. M. S. Richards outlined the first five steps that lead to having received a new heart and Christ living within. He then named the sixth step—baptism. After citing Romans 6:3-6, he commented, "When we read this passage we see how wonderful baptism is, and we never have any more doubts about its being necessary . . . . It is so important for us that Jesus took . . . [this sixth step] before a great multitude of people that we might have His blessed example to follow."

He added: "Baptism actually puts you up on the seventh step." Quoting 1 Corinthians 12:13, "For by one Spirit are we all baptized into one body," he commented, "That 'one body' mentioned here is the church. Some people say, 'Why, I want to be baptized and not belong to the church.' But they say that because they do not understand things properly." He clarified his position that it is not biblical to be baptized without joining the church by referring to Acts 2:37, 38, 41. "What happened to these people who believed? They were baptized. Did they hold back? No! They wanted to know what to do next. And then what happened to them? Did they just wander about like sheep with no shepherd? No indeed. Read verse 47, 'And the Lord added to the church daily such as should be saved.' Where did the Lord put them? He added them to the church. And let us not say that the Lord made a mistake. . . . He put them in the church. That's the seventh step on the Golden Stairs" that lead to the Golden City.

WHAT BAPTISM SYMBOLIZES.

The New Testament presents baptism within the context of Calvary, thus giving meaning and significance to this rite. First it symbolizes forgiveness of and death to sin.

Complete the following analysis chart of Romans 6:3-10 in order to recognize the symbolic aspect of baptism:

Symbol	Jesus	Us
Crucifixion	Crucified for our sins.	Old man (body of_____) crucified.
Death	Died for us.	Buried with Him by_____
Resurrection	Raised from the dead.	Raised in the_____ of His resurrection.
New Life	Lives unto God.	_____from sin; _____with Him

Repentant sinners identify themselves with Jesus through the rite of baptism. By the sinless life He lived, and by His death on behalf of sinners, Jesus made His righteousness available to all. By taking part in this ceremony that symbolizes the death and burial of the old life of sin, and resurrection to new life in Jesus, believers demonstrate their acceptance of Christ's righteousness and their entrance into newness of life.

What kind of relationship with Jesus is implied in such expressions in Romans 6:3, 4 as "baptized into Jesus Christ" and "buried with him by baptism"?

"The postbaptismal life is to be a new life, a different life, a life dead to sin and alive to God ([Romans 6:] verse 11, RSV). It is the life of one who has entered into a covenant relationship with God, who shares covenant fellowship with like believers and has pledged to adhere to the covenant stipulations. 'I will be their God, and they shall be my people' (Jer. 31:33, RSV)."—George Rice, "What Baptism Means to Me," *Adventist Review,* Dec. 11, 1986, p. 15.

When Jesus was baptized, the Holy Spirit descended upon Him in the form of a dove (see Matt. 3:16, 17). When we are baptized we may not see the dove descending, but in faith we know that God does for us what He did for Christ.

Following baptism, what does the Holy Spirit do for and in us? John 16:13, 14; Gal. 5:22-25.

WHAT BAPTISM INVOLVES.

Immersion in water. The Bible teaches baptism by immersion. In Romans and Colossians Paul compares the rite to Christ's death, burial, and resurrection. (See Rom. 6:1-6; compare Col. 2:12, 13.) This symbolism would have had no such significance if the apostolic church had practiced a mode of baptism other than immersion.

How do the passages that follow support baptism by immersion?

Matt. 3:16 _____

John 3:23 _____

Acts 8:38, 39 _____

"That immersion was the mode employed in NT times is clear from the meaning of the Greek term, from Bible descriptions of the performance of the ceremony, and from the spiritual applications made in the Bible respecting the rite. The term *baptizo* was used anciently to describe the immersing of cloth in dye, and of the submerging of a vessel in order to fill it with water. Its most obvious meaning when applied to Christian baptism is 'to immerse.'"—*SDA Bible Dictionary*, p. 119.

What experience must precede baptism? Acts 2:37, 38. How does this exclude infant baptism?

Infants are incapable of repentance, of deciding to be disciples or to obey God's will. Only baptism of believers who have reached the age of accountability and can "be born again" is indicated by the baptisms recorded in the New Testament. (See Acts 8:12, "both men and women"; Acts 8:13, Simon; Acts 8:29-39, the Ethiopian eunuch; Acts 9:17, 18, Saul; 1 Cor. 1:14, Crispus and Gaius.) Because individuals differ in the area of spiritual maturity, no fixed minimum age for baptism is set.

What about rebaptism? (See Acts 19:1-5.) The believers in Ephesus were rebaptized when they received greater light. This does not mean that we should be rebaptized every time we receive additional light, but it does establish a precedent for rebaptism of those who have not been living up to the light they have received and wish to testify to all that they have made a decision to begin a new life with Christ.

HOW WE PREPARE FOR BAPTISM.

"When a person acknowledges his lost state as a sinner, sincerely repents of his sins, and experiences conversion, he may, when properly instructed, be accepted as a proper candidate for baptism and church membership."—*SDA Church Manual* (1986), p. 42.

What are we to teach people in connection with Christ's commission to baptize them? Matt. 28:20.

All Christ's teachings are to be taught. "It is fully as important to teach men to observe the things Christ has commanded as it is to baptize. . . . Without the exercise of the mental faculties to understand the revealed will of God, there can be no real Christianity, no real growth. Instruction is thus of vital importance before and after baptism. . . . Nothing is to be omitted. It is not for man to declare that some of Christ's teachings are outmoded."—*SDA Bible Commentary*, vol. 5, pp. 557, 558.

What reactions to Bible teaching must precede baptism?

Acts 8:12 _____

Acts 8:35-38 _____

Acts 18:8 _____

Jesus made it clear that baptism is not an option, nor is it to be taken lightly. Baptism indicates a dramatic change in the direction of a person's life. (See Acts 8:36-38.) In the same way that baptism prepared people for Jesus' first coming, baptism helps prepare Jesus' loved ones for His second coming.

When the armies of the Roman Empire invaded Britain, they were commanded to burn their ships behind them. A soldier asked the commander, "Sir, how will we retreat if we burn the ships?" The commander's reply was, "That's the whole point; there will be no retreat!" As we enter into baptism by immersion we commit ourselves never to turn back to our old way of life. Now Jesus is supreme in our hearts.

As I think back about having been baptized or look forward to being baptized, what is most important to me about this rite, and what can I do to keep my commitment fresh and alive?

FURTHER STUDY: Arguments over the meaning of baptism and the age when a person should be baptized go back to an early period in the Christian church. Through the centuries many Christians have taught that infants must be baptized in order to be relieved of original guilt inherited from Adam. It is believed that if the unbaptized infant dies he is confined to "limbo," a halfway place in which he experiences neither the full joys of heaven nor the full terrors of hell. Others believe that by baptism the infant is incorporated into one "body" (1 Cor. 12:13) and clothed with Christ (Gal. 3:27). The Bible does not teach the concept of original guilt, and it teaches believer's baptism rather than infant baptism. We find ourselves in agreement with those churches that teach and practice immersion of believers.

The supreme proof of both the necessity and method of baptism is the example of Jesus, who in love was baptized to fulfill all righteousness and who endured an unparalleled baptism of suffering.

DISCUSSION QUESTIONS:

1. Do you realize that your sinless Lord, who did not need baptism, was baptized as an example for you to follow? If you have not yet done so, what do you intend to do as the Spirit leads you to follow His example in all things?

2. The thief on the cross was promised salvation by Christ but apparently was not baptized. What do you think he would have done in this matter if he had been able to come down from the cross?

3. Are you daily experiencing the burial of sinful living and a resurrection walk with Christ? How can you cooperate with the Holy Spirit as He works to ensure that this experience will be yours?

SUMMARY: When by faith a person experiences the new birth and is clothed with Christ's righteousness, as a new believer he or she should accept the rite of baptism by immersion as a testimony of union with Christ. In doing so, he or she becomes part of His body, the church. Because baptism focuses on the death, burial, and resurrection of Christ, it symbolizes that the believer has died to self and the world by the power of the Holy Spirit, and has made a full surrender to Christ and His will.

Lesson 15

The Lord's Supper

ARE YOU REMEMBERING JESUS? How do Christian believers today keep constantly in mind the significance of Christ's death, resurrection, and ascension to heaven? How do they enter into the spiritual experience enjoyed by Jesus' first disciples?

Christ designed the celebration of the Lord's Supper as one means by which those who believe might receive regular spiritual renewal. In everyday life, one effective way to get to know people is to eat with them. In the Lord's Supper not only do Christians eat together, they also commune with the Lord Jesus Christ. As they partake of the symbols of His sacrifice, they receive by faith the spiritual nourishment that only Jesus can supply.

Our concern in this lesson is to discover from the Bible what Jesus intends the Lord's Supper to mean to every Christian believer. We also need to know how to prepare our hearts to take part in this important service.

KEY THOUGHT. In the Lord's Supper we partake of the symbols of Christ's sacrifice as an expression of faith in Him. The foot-washing service signifies spiritual cleansing preparatory to renewing fellowship with Christ.

> **"The cup of blessing which we bless, is it not the communion of the blood of Christ? The bread which we break, is it not the communion of the body of Christ? For we being many are one bread, and one body: for we are all partakers of that one bread" (1 Corinthians 10:16, 17).**

THE IMPORTANCE OF HUMBLE SERVICE.

What problem kept recurring among Jesus' disciples? Mark 9:33, 34.

There were only a few hours left before Jesus would be cruelly crucified. Yet in the upper room pride ruled. The disciples were vying with one another for the highest place in the kingdom. They had not learned the lesson of unselfish service. When group photographs are taken some stand to one side while wishing for a center position in the front row. So with the twelve; questions of status and personal importance were supreme. They wanted to be served instead of being servants. Try to imagine the feelings of Jesus in this situation.

How did Jesus emphasize the importance of humility? Matt. 18:1-4; 20:25-28.

Before honor is humility. Love for reward, position, or distinction has no place in Christ's kingdom. Rank, wealth, beauty, or intellectual greatness can never be substitutes for union with the humble Christ. People do not have rank in Christ's spiritual kingdom because they are physically attractive; nor are they given special honor or position because they are important. The qualification for service in the church, Jesus taught, is noble character and commitment to unselfish service. Only those with changed hearts can understand these principles—"Except ye be converted" (Matt. 18:3). In God's sight, the greatest person in the church is the one who renders the most humble service, motivated by love for Christ and for others.

"Had Christ come in the majesty of a king, with the pomp which attends the great men of earth, many would have accepted Him. But Jesus of Nazareth did not dazzle the senses with a display of outward glory and make this the foundation of their reverence. He came as a humble man to be the Teacher and Exemplar as well as the Redeemer of the race. Had He encouraged pomp, had He come followed by a retinue of great men of earth, how could He have taught humility?"—Ellen G. White, *Testimonies*, vol. 5, p. 253.

How would you define humility? What place should self-respect have in the attitudes of the Christian? When does self-respect become pride?

THE ORDINANCE OF HUMILITY.

The night before Jesus' death the disciples were arguing about which one of them was the greatest. Jesus could not lead them into a spiritual service with sin in their hearts. So He did something special to teach them humility.

What demonstration of love and humility did Jesus give His disciples at the Last Supper? John 13:1-7.

While contention for the highest place reigned in the upper room, Jesus knelt down and washed the soiled feet of His disciples. He stooped to serve.

Think of the emotions that must have surged through Judas's mind as Jesus washed his feet. For thirty pieces of silver Judas was about to hand Jesus over to the Jewish authorities. Nevertheless, the Messiah, who knew what Judas had done, instead of exposing him, stooped to wash his feet. Christ's love brought powerful conviction for Judas to confess his sin. Tragically, Judas rejected it.

Peter's reaction was different. He was overwhelmed by His Lord's bending so low as to wash his feet. He was ashamed that he was not doing what Jesus was doing. He sensed that his personal pride had kept him from being a servant. (See *The Desire of Ages*, pp. 645, 646.)

Of what is the washing of feet a symbol? John 13:8-11; 15:3; Titus 3:5-7.

The washing of the disciples' feet symbolized the spiritual cleansing that only Christ can provide—the washing away of our sins. This cleansing He wanted them to accept as the preparation for the Lord's Supper.

What did Jesus urge His followers to do for one another? John 13:12-17.

Foot washing is a vital preparation for the communion service. Jesus said, "You also ought to wash one another's feet. For I have given you an example, that you also should do as I have done to you" (John 13:14, 15, RSV).

Why does washing the feet of an antagonist help bring about reconciliation and acceptance?

THE INSTITUTION OF THE LORD'S SUPPER.

Describe the service that Jesus instituted after He had washed the disciples' feet. Matt. 26:26-28.

The last meal that Jesus ate with His disciples on the Thursday evening before His crucifixion was the celebration of the Passover. (See John 13:1.) What Christians call the Last Supper was Jesus' last Passover. The Passover pointed forward to the sacrifice of the Messiah for the sins of the world. (See 1 Cor. 5:7.) The next day, after the Passover supper, Jesus was crucified. Then the Old Testament sanctuary services that pointed forward to His death lost their significance. Animal sacrifices were replaced by the true Sacrifice, and earthly ministry gave place to the heavenly High Priestly ministry of Jesus. (See Heb. 10:11, 12; 7:25.)

This is why at the Last Supper Jesus instituted another service, the Lord's Supper, to take the place of the Passover. The communion service spans the gulf between Calvary and the Second Advent. The Passover pointed *forward* to Calvary, while the Lord's Supper points *back* to Calvary. Thus the Lord's Supper commemorates three events: (1) The completed sacrifice on the cross; (2) the coming of Jesus the second time, and (3) the final triumph of God's people in the heavenly kingdom.

How do we know that Jesus wants His followers to celebrate the Lord's Supper until He comes the second time? 1 Cor. 11:23-26. What danger is there in partaking of the Lord's Supper if your heart is not right with God? 1 Cor. 11:27-30.

The Lord's Supper is designed to remind us of Christ's death until His second advent (1 Cor. 11:26). The Bible does not tell us how often the service should be celebrated. In the Seventh-day Adventist Church we celebrate it once a quarter—four times a year. The reason for this is that we do not want the service to become a commonplace formality, as could happen if we celebrated it more often; nor do we want the service to be an incidental part of the life of the church, as it could become if we celebrated it less often.

The apostle Paul's stern warning emphasizes our great need of spiritual preparation for the Lord's Supper. How can we prepare our hearts for this special event?

THE SPIRITUAL MEANING OF THE LORD'S SUPPER.

What does it mean to partake of the body and blood of Christ?

John 6:51, 53-57, 63 _____

1 Cor. 10:16, 17 _____

When Jesus spoke of believers' partaking of His flesh and drinking His blood, He was speaking metaphorically. The disciples did not eat the literal body of Christ at the Last Supper, nor did they drink His literal blood. The unleavened bread and the unfermented wine *represent* the spiritual life from Christ that the Holy Spirit imparts when we partake of His written Word.

In His great sermon on the Bread of Life (John 6), Jesus clarified beyond doubt what it means to partake of His body and blood. "It is the spirit that gives life, the flesh is of no avail; the words that I have spoken to you are spirit and life" (John 6:63, RSV). We partake of Christ's body and blood when we receive His Word and His Spirit into our hearts. (See Rom. 8:9, 10; Eph. 3:16-21.)

How many times was Jesus sacrificed for our sins? Is the Lord's Supper a repetition of the sacrifice of Calvary? Heb. 7:27; 9:28; 10:14.

Only once was it necessary for Jesus to be sacrificed for human guilt. The suffering that atoned for sin was not primarily physical. It was the suffering of the Deity caused by the separation of God the Son from the Father and the Holy Spirit. This separation broke the heart of the Son of God. That one sacrifice was sufficient to atone for all sin for as long as this old world continues. The punishment Christ bore is adequate for all sinners no matter how degraded—if they will open their hearts and accept Jesus as Saviour and Lord. (See Rom. 5:17.)

The celebration of the Lord's Supper does not repeat Calvary; it reminds us of the enormous sacrifice made for our salvation. As we contemplate the final scenes of Christ's life, His Word becomes more precious to us and, by His Spirit, He fills our hearts.

What changes in our world were the direct result of Christ's death for our sins? What difference has Calvary made to you personally?

17

When did Jesus say the next occasion would be on which He would celebrate the Lord's Supper with His followers? Matt. 26:29.

In explaining the significance of the fruit of the vine partaken by the disciples in the first Lord's Supper service, Jesus said: "This is my blood of the covenant, which is poured out for many for the forgiveness of sins" (Matt. 26:28, NIV). The covenant He spoke of is the everlasting covenant of righteousness and salvation by faith. Under this covenant, because of His one sacrifice, His will is written on the hearts of those who believe, they are given eternal life, and they will be taken to the heavenly kingdom at His coming. (See Heb. 8:8-12.)

This is why in the very next verse (Matt. 26:29) Jesus directs our attention to the fruition of the covenant relationship. In the heavenly kingdom He will partake with us of the symbol of His sacrifice, because then the purpose of the covenant will be completely fulfilled. Sinners will be transformed into saints, enjoying the perfection and immortality that Jesus made possible by bearing the punishment for their sins.

What are the qualifications necessary for those who will feast with Jesus in the heavenly kingdom? Rev. 19:7-9.

Jesus is waiting to drink of the fruit of the vine at the "marriage supper of the Lamb" (Rev. 19:9), when the triumph of His plan of salvation will be celebrated. Every time we celebrate the Lord's Supper, Christ is with us by the Holy Spirit. But our sights are to be set on the future when God's people will be free from sin and all its results.

Those who by faith receive and retain the free gift of Christ's righteousness will be taken to His heavenly kingdom to enjoy the ultimate Lord's Supper. Christ's righteousness dwells within believers as they allow the Holy Spirit to reign within. (See Col. 1:27; Rev. 3:20.) Every time we partake of the Lord's Supper in the scriptural manner, we receive Jesus by faith, and He becomes our indwelling righteousness, our qualification for the heavenly kingdom.

Why is it vitally important for Christians to keep the heavenly kingdom in view? What difference does this make in their lives in the here and now?

FURTHER STUDY: What similarities do you see between the significance of the manna and shewbread in ancient Israel and the bread and wine partaken of by New Testament Christians? (See Lev. 24:5-9; Deut. 8:3, 16; Neh. 9:19-21; John 6:27-63; Rev. 2:17.)

Read "A Servant of Servants" in *The Desire of Ages*, pp. 642-661.

Discuss the following passages that reveal the correct attitude to and the correct manner of celebrating the Lord's Supper:

1. The Lord's Supper is to be a joyous, blessed occasion. 1 Cor. 10:16: The story of the cross is the most exciting news for all mankind. At the birth of Jesus the angels sang, "Glory to God in the highest, and on earth peace, good will toward men" (Luke 2:14). The glory, peace, and goodwill are possible because Jesus died for our sins.

2. Believers should be present and partake of the Supper as members of the body of Christ. 1 Cor. 10:17: Because we are all members of the body of Christ, if possible we should be present when His death is celebrated. If we are absent, we deny ourselves the special blessing the Lord has for us.

3. All Jesus' followers who wish to take part should be invited. Matt. 26:27: As we have seen, the Lord instructs us to be spiritually prepared before partaking of the Lord's Supper. But whether a person is spiritually prepared is a matter for his or her own conscience. Christ allowed Judas to partake of the Last Supper and used the occasion as an opportunity to make a final appeal to his heart.

4. Only unfermented wine is to be used. Prov. 20:1: Jesus did not act in any manner contrary to His Word. The wine He used at the Last Supper was unfermented grape juice (Matt. 26:29). Fermented wine could never have represented the purity of Christ's sacrifice.

5. Only unleavened bread should be used. 1 Cor. 5:7, 8: Leaven represents sin. "Therefore let us keep the feast, not with the old leaven, neither with the leaven of malice and wickedness; but with the unleavened bread of sincerity and truth." Paul wrote this after the Passover service had lost its significance; he spoke of the Lord's Supper.

SUMMARY: We appeal to all who have not yet done so to give their hearts to Jesus, allowing Him to reign in their lives by the Holy Spirit, so that they can be happy participants in the Lord's Supper.

Lesson 16

Spiritual Gifts

JESUS' PROVISION FOR HIS CHURCH: Circumstances sometimes make it necessary for families to be separated for long periods. Often the separation is occasioned by the necessity for the husband and father to travel in the interests of his profession, sometimes being away for many months. If he is a responsible person, he will make certain that his family is well cared for during his absence.

Nineteen centuries ago, after establishing His church on earth, Jesus returned to heaven. With anxious hearts the disciples watched Him ascend. (See Luke 24:50, 51; Acts 1:9.) Would they be able to represent Him adequately? Would they have the talents needed to carry the gospel to all the world?

Jesus foresaw their needs and made full provision for them. Through the gift of the Holy Spirit, He provided for the needs of His disciples and church from the time of His ascension until He would return again. But the greatest outpouring of the Holy Spirit is yet to be received. It will be given as soon as the church is ready to facilitate the finishing of God's work in the world.

KEY THOUGHT: Through the agency of the Holy Spirit, God bestows on all members of His church in every age spiritual gifts that each member is to employ in loving ministry for the common good of the church and of humanity.

"Wherefore he saith, When he ascended up on high, he led captivity captive, and gave gifts unto men" (Eph. 4:8).

THE PROMISE FULFILLED.

Summarize in your own words Jesus' last promise to the disciples recorded in Acts 1:5, 8. When was this promise realized by the infant church? Eph. 4:8, Acts 2:1-4.

The promise brought dynamic power for witnessing. The Holy Spirit is given to the church to enable it to fulfill its mission. It is the Spirit alone that can make our witnessing effective. While remaining in the upper room where they had partaken of the Last Supper, the disciples prepared for the reception of the promised Holy Spirit.

What was the result of their preparations? "They were weighted with the burden of the salvation of souls. They realized that the gospel was to be carried to the world, and they claimed the power that Christ had promised. . . . The Spirit came upon the waiting, praying disciples with a fullness that reached every heart. The Infinite One revealed Himself in power to His church. It was as if for ages this influence had been held in restraint, and now Heaven rejoiced in being able to pour out upon the church the riches of the Spirit's grace."—Ellen G. White, *The Acts of the Apostles*, pp. 37, 38.

In what spectacular way was the prayer of the disciples for power to win souls answered? Acts 2:41.

It must have been difficult for the early church with its primitive organization to keep up with the spectacular growth that took place:

Acts 2:41—3,000 baptized in one day.

Acts 2:47—Members added daily.

Acts 4:4—5,000 men (no mention of how many women or children) who heard and believed the message.

Acts 4:32—A multitude believed.

Acts 5:14—Multitudes added to the church.

Acts 5:28—The apostles accused of filling Jerusalem with their doctrine.

Acts 6:7—A great company of priests converted.

In the light of the promise of the outpouring of the latter rain in Joel 2:28, 29, what would happen if we today followed the same steps that the disciples took before Pentecost? (Read "Pentecost" in Ellen G. White's *The Acts of the Apostles*, especially pages 36, 37.)

How did Paul indicate that it is important for us to understand all we can about spiritual gifts? 1 Cor. 12:1.

Study the chart that follows in order to gain a fuller understanding of what Paul includes in his listing of spiritual gifts:

Paul's List of Spiritual Gifts				
Rom. 12:6-8	Eph. 4:7-11	1 Cor. 12:4-11	1 Cor. 12:28-31	1 Cor. 13:1-3

1. Prophecy
2. Ministry
3. Teaching
4. Exhorting
5. Giving
6. Ruling
7. Showing
   mercy
8. Tongues
	1. Apostles
	2. Prophets
	3. Evangelists
	4. Pastor-
	   teachers
		1. Wisdom
		2. Knowledge
		3. Faith
		4. Healing
		5. Miracles
		6. Prophecy
		7. Discerning
		   spirits
		8. Tongues
		9. Interpretation
		   of tongues
			1. Apostles
			2. Prophets
			3. Teachers
			4. Miracles
			5. Healings
			6. Helps
			7. Governments
				1. Martyrdom
				2. Sacrifice
				3. Faith
				4. Knowledge
				5. Prophecy
				6. Tongues

Not one of these lists is complete. How many separate gifts can you find in Paul's outline?

In the Greek, Ephesians 4:11 indicates that when Paul listed "pastors and teachers" he was not talking about two separate gifts, but one. That is why these are listed on one line in the chart and hyphenated.

Notice that Paul's lists seem to vary because of the different reasons that he had in mind for listing the gifts in each passage mentioned. In Romans 12 his emphasis is on the *usefulness* of the gifts listed. In Ephesians 4 there seems to be an attempt to list the order of *importance* to the church. In 1 Corinthians 12:4-11 Paul stresses the *communication* factor involved. Later in this same chapter he apparently lists the gifts in order of importance once again. When we put the list found in 1 Corinthians 13 in inverted order (as in the chart), a listing of order of importance also becomes apparent, although his emphasis in this chapter is on the *lasting effects* of the gifts.

Which gift appears in each of these lists? Why is that significant to us today?

WHAT IS THE PURPOSE OF THE GIFTS?

What major purpose for the spiritual gifts do you see in Ephesians 4:2, 3, 12, 13?

What God wishes to accomplish through the gifts. The gifts enumerated by Paul include "helps, giving, and showing mercy." Note how these can be applied in a practical way. "Some time ago my wife led a church youth group that wanted to do something significant for the community. Someone suggested that since several wealthy people lived in the community along with many others with needs, it might be possible to match the needs with some of that affluence.

"The youth divided into two groups. One went door-to-door to the wealthy section of town asking what the people had that they might be willing to give away. The other half went to the less privileged part of the city to ask what the people needed.

"A couple of hours later the two groups reconvened at the church and compared notes. What were the needs? What were the resources? Excitement reigned. Here was a mother in need of food for her baby, and here a family that had baby food left over after the visit of grandchildren. Here was a family who had no kitchen table, and another who had replaced theirs and had no room to store the old one.

"Although the story is true, I see it also as a parable of what God wishes to accomplish in His church through the miracle of spiritual gifts. The Christian church is a place where people can come to get help—of whatever kind."—Don Jacobsen, "What Spiritual Gifts Mean to Me," *Adventist Review*, Dec. 25, 1986, pp. 11, 12.

List as many purposes for the gifts as you can from Paul's discussion in Ephesians 4:12, 14, 15:

1. _____

2. _____

3. _____

4. _____

What indication does Paul give that the gifts still are necessary in our day? Eph. 4:13.

HOW DO THE GIFTS RANK IN IMPORTANCE?

Why does the Spirit give different gifts to the members of the body of Christ? 1 Cor. 12:11-25.

Although Paul shows the value of each distinct gift, there is a sense in 1 Corinthians 12 through 14 in which some gifts are said to be more important than others. (See 1 Cor. 12:31.) He demonstrates that the tongues phenomenon that was taking place in the Corinthian church should not be given undue importance. (See 1 Corinthians 14.)

Notice that the gift of tongues rated low on the scale of importance assigned. Instead of condemning the manifestation of tongues in Corinth, Paul pointed out that there is a "more excellent way" (1 Cor. 12:31). In 1 Corinthians 13 he stated that none of the gifts has real value unless combined with the gift of love.

Compare Paul's lists of what love is and what it is not in 1 Corinthians 13. How does such a comparison help us understand more fully the kind of love about which the apostle is talking? If possible, use a newer translation.

What contrast is drawn between love and such gifts as prophecy, knowledge, and tongues in 1 Corinthians 13:8-12?

There are three particularly valuable and abiding gifts given to all who accept Christ: (1) faith, (2) hope, and (3) love. Love is the most important and significant gift.

The two Pentecosts. The Bible teaches that there are two major outpourings of the Holy Spirit. The first was given to the church at Pentecost and has never been taken away. That first outpouring (called the early rain) continues in the church through the daily, hourly work of the Spirit in our lives, bringing about transformation and victory over sin, covering us with Christ's righteousness.

When we take full advantage of the perfecting power of the early rain, the lovely character of Christ will be seen in us. The soul temple will be cleansed from "every defilement. Then the latter rain will fall upon us as the early rain fell on the disciples on the day of Pentecost" (Ellen G. White, *Testimonies*, vol. 5, p. 214). The latter rain will be poured out as a means of calling the attention of the world to the love of God evidenced in His church.

DISCOVERING YOUR GIFTS.

What indicates that every church member has a gift or gifts? 1 Cor. 12:4-11.

Every member has at least one gift. But not all receive the same gift. Note that the Spirit decides which gifts to bestow. He alone knows which gifts are needed by the church. Therefore we need to discover for ourselves which gift or gifts the Spirit has given each of us.

How do we discover which gift or gifts God has given us? Don Jacobsen lists the following suggestions to help discover God's gifts in himself and in others:

"1. **Walk closely with Jesus each day.** Spiritual gifts are for spiritual people. Sometimes I have felt like doing nothing in Christ's service because I have grown careless in my walk with Him.

"2. **Gather a group of fellow believers,** perhaps including your pastor, and carefully study the biblical topic of spiritual gifts. This extremely important step will help inform later decisions.

"3. **Be willing to venture and experiment.** If you sense a gentle nudge of the Spirit, or are asked to undertake a new and unfamiliar task in your church or community, don't immediately say 'No.' If it frightens you, ask whether you could try it for a month rather than a year, as an associate rather than the leader.

"4. **After you have some experience, consult your own feelings.** God-appointed service, done in His way, will bring great satisfaction. While you may not feel adequate or capable, you should find a sense of accomplishment in knowing that you are using tools crafted especially for you.

"5. **Look for affirmation from other Spirit-led Christians.** If God has called and gifted you for some area of service, others of His family will notice. Often in this setting God will confirm your gift. On the other hand, if you receive no response, see no fruit, and feel constant drudgery in the task, perhaps God wishes to call you to a different area of ministry.

"God equips His Spirit-filled people to be the channels through whom He can pour the rich resources of heaven upon those in need—in the church and out. One of the most thrilling discoveries a Christian can make is to see God's kingdom extended and humbly acknowledge, 'God used me there.' "
—Jacobsen, *Adventist Review*, Dec. 25, 1986, pp. 12, 13.

FURTHER STUDY: During the past few years the subject of spiritual gifts has been a dominant theme in the evangelical world. It is a common subject taught in numerous church seminaries. Seminars dealing with spiritual gifts are being conducted regularly, teaching what spiritual gifts are and how to use them. In some groups, spiritual gifts seem to focus mainly on speaking in tongues. Speaking in tongues, however, is not limited to any one group. It forms what might be termed a religious cross-cultural phenomenon. Not all manifestations of "tongues" are from heaven. In a world where the supernatural is promoted, Christians must be certain to base their beliefs about spiritual gifts exclusively on the Scriptures.

Study the parable of the talents in Matthew 25:14-30. How do they relate to our study of the spiritual gifts?

"The special gifts of the Spirit are not the only talents represented in the parable [of the talents]. It includes all gifts and endowments, whether original or acquired, natural or spiritual. All are to be employed in Christ's service."—Ellen G. White, *Christ's Object Lessons*, p. 328.

DISCUSSION QUESTIONS:

1. Not all are given the same gifts. As has been developed in this lesson, the genuine gift of tongues is one of the lesser gifts in the order of importance Paul presents. How would you help those who give undue emphasis to the gift of tongues understand what the Bible teaches on this matter?

2. How does this study of the gifts of the Spirit relate to you personally? Do you daily pray for God to give you the gift of fitness to meet others in a redemptive way?

3. Do you realize that the remnant church, as the body of Christ, will be known not so much for what it teaches as for how it lives? In what ways is the Holy Spirit helping you live for Christ?

SUMMARY: Spiritual gifts are given to build up the church to spiritual maturity, to foster unity of the faith and knowledge of God, and to enable believers to share their faith with others. Some members are called by God and endowed by the Spirit for functions recognized by the church in pastoral, evangelistic, apostolic, and teaching ministries particularly needed to equip the members for service. All members receive some gift to be used to glorify God and further the work of the body of Christ.

Lesson 17

The Gift of Prophecy

HOW CAN WE IDENTIFY TRUE PROPHETS? We can be grateful that God chose prophets in past ages to present special messages to His people (2 Peter 1:20, 21). But Jesus predicted that in the last days there would arise "false Christs, and false prophets" (Matt 24:24). False religious teachers, people claiming to be Christ, and others claiming to have received direct communications from God are prevalent in our contemporary world.

Every Christian should be able to distinguish the false from the true. The Bible says much about the work of true prophets and the means by which they can be identified.

Since God gave special messages through the prophets in the past, why can He not use someone in that way in the twentieth century? Is God's power to communicate with His people any less today than it was in the time of Elijah or Jeremiah? Why should we accept the reality of miraculous prophetic inspiration in earlier ages but deny it for our age? If we should discover that the tests of a true prophet are fulfilled in the ministry of an individual in modern times, how unwise we would be not to accept his or her messages as coming from God! To reject the counsel of a true prophet is to insult the Holy Spirit.

KEY THOUGHT. Special revelations from God come to humankind through prophets. The Bible gives us tests by which we can determine whether a professed prophet is of God.

> **"Believe in the Lord your God, so shall ye be established; believe his prophets, so shall ye prosper" (2 Chronicles 20:20).**

27

What do the following Bible passages tell us about the work of Bible prophets?

Luke 24:27 _____

2 Tim. 3:16, 17 _____

1 Peter 1:10, 11 _____

The central purpose of all divine prophecy is the revelation of Jesus Christ as the only way of salvation. Prophets taught, warned, and encouraged, as well as often predicted the future.

Sometimes the instruction given has timeless relevance. It is intended not only for the prophet's day but also for every subsequent age. Sometimes the messages were intended for the prophet's contemporaries. In such cases, the messages were not preserved for our age. (See 1 Chron. 29:29, 30.) The writings of such prophets as Nathan, Gad, Ahijah, and Jehu are not in the sacred canon (the collection of Bible books) evidently because they did not have special application for future generations.

The Lord has sometimes chosen prophets to meet local situations. For instance, the Spirit of the Lord came upon Jahaziel, who prophesied before the people of Judah during the reign of Jehoshaphat. He assured them of victory over their enemies the next day. (See 2 Chron. 20:15.)

An inspired prophet is not necessarily a canonical prophet—one whose messages are recorded in the canon of Scripture. But the messages of noncanonical prophets came from God, just as did the messages of canonical prophets.

The Lord does not discriminate on the basis of gender when choosing persons to communicate His special messages to the people. Women as well as men were called to the prophetic office. Name some women in the Bible who were prophets.

Judges 4:4, 5 _____

2 Kings 22:14 _____

Luke 2:36 _____

Acts 21:9 _____

In what main ways did God's messages come to the prophets?

Hosea 12:10 _____

Dan. 7:1 _____

Dan. 8:16, 17 _____

Eze. 2:2, 3 _____

Prophets sometimes heard audibly direct communications of the Holy Spirit, while at other times they received unmistakable inner commands. There was direct communication from the mind of God to the mind of the prophet, as God communicated a specific divine message. The prophet communicated this message.

"It is not the words of the Bible that are inspired, but the men that were inspired. Inspiration acts not on the man's words or his expressions but on the man himself, who, under the influence of the Holy Ghost, is imbued with thoughts. But the words receive the impress of the individual mind. The divine mind is diffused. The divine mind and will is combined with the human mind and will; thus the utterances of the man are the word of God."—Ellen G. White, *Selected Messages*, book 1, p. 21.

What physical state did the prophet sometimes experience when in vision? Dan. 10:7-9, 16-19; Num. 24:3, 4, 16; 2 Cor. 12:1-4.

The Bible does not teach that the physical state of the prophet while in vision was always the same. Nor are we told that the physical phenomena are to be used as a test of the genuineness of a prophet's claims. Satan can counterfeit the physical state of the prophet in vision. If the physical phenomena are present when other Bible tests of a true prophet give positive results, they can be regarded as supporting evidence of the genuineness of the gift.

In what two ways did prophets pass on God's messages to the people? Isa. 6:9-11; Jer. 36:1, 2.

Which Bible prophet's messages have you found to be especially relevant to your need?

With what teachings will the true prophet's messages be consistent? Isa. 8:20; Rev. 22:18, 19 (compare Jer. 23:16, 21, 22, 28).

Isaiah 8:20 is translated in the New International Version: "To the law and to the testimony! If they do not speak according to this word, they have no light of dawn." If they do not teach according to the Bible, then you know that their message did not come from God.

"The word of God is the standard by which all teaching and experience must be tested."

"God will have a people upon the earth to maintain the Bible, and the Bible only, as the standard of all doctrines and the basis of all reforms."—Ellen G. White, *The Great Controversy*, pp. vii, 595.

"The Bible, and the Bible alone, is to be our creed, the sole bond of union; all who bow to this Holy Word will be in harmony."—Ellen G. White, *Selected Messages*, book 1, p. 416.

What will be the spiritual results of a true prophet's teaching in his own life and in the lives of those he or she influences? Matt. 7:15-20.

One of the major signs of the end will be false prophets whose main work is deception. (See Matt. 24:4, 11, 24.) Christ has given His true followers the right to be fruit-inspectors: "By their fruit you will recognize them" (Matt. 7:20, NIV).

How reliable are the predictions of a true prophet of God? Deut. 18:20-22; Jer. 28:9.

Some divine predictions are conditional upon the people's response. God saved Nineveh despite Jonah's predictions that He would destroy it. The people fulfilled the condition for the divine sentence to be waived. (See Jonah 3:10.) God could not fulfill many of the divine promises to literal Israel because of the people's continuing apostasy. (See Jer. 18:7-10.) Nevertheless, the test is valid—true prophets do not make false predictions.

What will the true prophet teach in regard to Jesus Christ? 1 John 4:1-3.

WILL THERE BE TRUE PROPHETS IN THE LAST DAYS?

What do the Bible passages that follow reveal about the gift of prophecy in the last-day church?

Joel 2:28-32 _____

Eph. 4:11-14 _____

Rev. 12:17 _____

Rev. 19:10 _____

Joel's prophecy establishes that in the last days some faithful ones will receive visions and dreams from the Lord. In his great sermon on the day of Pentecost, the apostle Peter stated that the outpouring of the Holy Spirit manifested then was a fulfillment of Joel's prophecy. (See Acts 2:16-21.) Although Pentecost was an initial fulfillment of Joel's prophecy, the final fulfillment will come a short time prior to the second coming of Christ. Notice that immediately after Joel's prediction of the outpouring of the Holy Spirit, he describes the events surrounding the second coming of Jesus (Joel 2:30-32).

Paul taught that the prophetic gift would be needed in the church "until we all attain to the unity of the faith and of the knowledge of the Son of God, to mature manhood, to the measure of the stature of the fulness of Christ" (Eph. 4:13, RSV). When God's people arrive at that spiritual condition, Jesus will come. (Compare Rev. 19:7-9.)

The "testimony of Jesus Christ" to which John refers in Revelation 12:17 is defined in Revelation 19:10. The angel who spoke these words clearly meant that, like John, he received prophetic messages from Christ. The point is that "the testimony of Jesus Christ" in the book of Revelation refers to more than the work of the Holy Spirit in every believing heart. It refers to the work of inspired prophets who, like John, have received visions, dreams, and special verbal communications to be given to humanity. (Compare Rev. 22:8, 9.) The Lord promised that He would give prophetic messages in the last days to lead people back to the Bible and back to Jesus.

What should be our attitude to the work of genuinely inspired prophets? 1 Thess. 5:19-21; 2 Chron. 20:20.

How willing would you be to listen to a modern prophet?

HAS THE PROPHETIC GIFT BEEN MANIFESTED IN THE LAST-DAY CHURCH?

The Seventh-day Adventist Church believes that the true gift of prophecy was manifested in the ministry of Ellen G. White. The questions that follow are suggested by the foregoing Bible study:

1. What did Ellen White claim for herself?

"I have had no claims to make, only that *I am instructed that I am the Lord's messenger*; that He called me in my youth to be His messenger, to receive His word, and to give a clear and decided message in the name of the Lord Jesus. . . .

"Why have I not claimed to be a prophet?—Because in these days many who boldly claim that they are prophets are a reproach to the cause of Christ; *and because my work includes much more than the word 'prophet' signifies*."—Ellen G. White, *Selected Messages*, book 1, p. 32 (italics supplied).

2. Did Ellen White claim to have visions and dreams from the Lord?

Many times in her writings she refers to visions and dreams given to her by God. (See *Testimonies*, vol. 1, pp. 58-61, 67-71, 72, 74, 76, 77, 79, 83.)

3. Does Ellen White measure up to the tests of a true prophet?

• **The consistency of her writings with Scripture**. Ellen White's writings teach no doctrine that cannot be substantiated solely from Scripture. Her writings lead us back to the Bible. They provide simple explanations of Bible truths that those professing to believe Scripture should have understood.

Ellen White did not teach that her writings should be used as another Bible or that they should be added to the sacred canon: "I recommend to you, dear reader, the Word of God as the rule of your faith and practice. By that Word we are to be judged. God has, in that Word, promised to give visions in the *'last days'*; not for a new rule of faith, but for the comfort of His people, and to correct those who err from Bible truth."—Ellen G. White, *Early Writings*, p. 78.

"Little heed is given to the Bible, and the Lord has given a lesser light to lead men and women to the greater light." —*Review and Herald*, Jan. 20, 1903, p. 15.

• **The fruitage of Ellen White's work.** The noble Christian character of Ellen White was attested to by many of those who knew her. (See Arthur L. White's biography entitled *Ellen G. White*, 6 volumes. These volumes are a rich source of information regarding the work of Ellen White. See also F. D. Nichol, *Ellen G. White and Her Critics*.)

The fruitage of Ellen White's work in the lives of others is demonstrated in two ways:

The growth of the Seventh-day Adventist work and institutions around the world: The Seventh-day Adventist Church has large and widespread educational, medical, and publishing work. This is mainly attributable to Ellen White's work as God's messenger.

The spiritual impact of her writings: Her published works have drawn millions to Christ and the Bible. The only way to test her influence for yourself is to read her works.

• **Ellen White's predictions have been accurate.** All of the unconditional predictions applying to the period prior to our day have been fulfilled. Current events reveal the gradual fulfillment of her predictions for the last days. (See the final chapters of *The Great Controversy*.) In 1848 she correctly predicted the amazing growth of the Seventh-day Adventist publishing work. (See *Life Sketches*, p. 125.) In the earliest stages of spiritualism's growth in America, she predicted that it would become a world religion. (See *Early Writings*, pp. 43, 59, 87.) In 1890 she predicted the destruction that came in two world wars. (See *Messages to Young People*, pp. 89, 90.)

Arthur L. White's six-volume biography of Ellen G. White provides convincing evidence that her predictions regarding the lives of individuals and the circumstances of the church have been remarkably fulfilled.

• **Ellen White exalted Christ.** Her writings exalt Christ as the only Source of salvation, the Head of the church, the all-sufficient Sacrifice, the forgiving Mediator, and the merciful Judge. She depicts Christ as Deity in the highest sense, and human in every respect except sin. (See *The Desire of Ages, Christ's Object Lessons, Thoughts From the Mount of Blessing*.) *Steps to Christ* is a superb commentary on the Bible teaching of righteousness by faith in Jesus.

FURTHER STUDY: Study how later inspired prophets provided authoritative interpretations of the writings of earlier prophets. See Rom. 10:6-10 (compare Deut. 30:11-14); Rom. 1:16, 17 (compare Hab. 2:4). Did Ellen White provide inspired interpretations of Scripture? See *Colporteur Ministry*, p. 126; *Testimonies*, vol. 8, p. 236; *Testimonies to Ministers*, p. 402; *Gospel Workers*, p. 302; *This Day With God*, p. 317.

SUMMARY: The Bible teaches that the genuineness of a professed prophet can be determined by applying the tests given in Scripture. When these tests are applied to Ellen White, she is found to be an inspired modern prophet.

Lesson 18

The Law of God

GOD'S LOVE IN HIS LAW. A man journeying by foot was puzzled yet amused by a sign he came across in front of a convent. It read: "KEEP OUT, SISTERS OF MERCY."

As he continued his travels he meditated on the apparent inconsistency. Some see an inconsistency between the Bible's emphasis on combining law with grace, faith with works, and justice with mercy. But there is none.

God thundered His love at Mt. Sinai. He expanded its meaning in the Sermon on the Mount. But He displayed its depth and fullness at Mt. Calvary. Sinai still symbolizes law and Calvary symbolizes grace. Yet one is not complete without the other. Sinai shows us what God's love is like and how far we are removed by nature from living a life that reflects His love. Calvary shows us that God's law could not be changed; thus God Himself had to pay the price for our sins.

KEY THOUGHT: The great principles of God's law are embodied in the Ten Commandments and exemplified in the life of Christ. They express God's love, will, and purposes concerning human conduct and relationships and are binding upon all people in every age. These precepts are the basis of God's covenant with His people and the standard of God's judgment.

> **"Do we then make void the law through faith? God forbid: yea, we establish the law" (Rom. 3:31).**

34

THE LAW REVEALS GOD'S LOVE.

God's law is eternal in principle. As the transcript of His character, it demonstrates what God's love is like.

Study the chart that follows, comparing the attributes of God with the inherent qualities of the law:

God	Attribute	Law
Ezra 9:15	Righteous	Ps. 119:172
Matt. 5:48	Perfect	Ps. 19:7
Lev. 19:2	Holy	Rom. 7:12
Ps. 34:8	Good	Rom. 7:12
Deut. 32:4	Truth	Ps. 119:142

How does Matthew 22:36-40 sum up the essence of the law?

Jesus made it clear that He did not come to change the law of God (Matt. 5:17). The first four of the Ten Commandments in Exodus 20:3-11 deal with our relationship to God. The last six in Exodus 20:12-17 are concerned primarily with our relationships with people about us.

"If man loves God in all the breadth and beauty suggested by the words 'with all thy heart, and with all thy soul, and with all thy mind,' he cannot possibly find room for another God. . . . Out of love will spring that hallowing of the name of God which will dry the springs of blasphemy, and make the double dealing of the hypocrite an impossibility. The Sabbath will be eagerly welcomed, and all its privileges earnestly and gladly appropriated. . . .

"Passing to the second table, and looking now at love in its working toward others, it will at once be seen that the only sufficient power for obedience and honor rendered to parents is that of love. There will be no thought of murder until the awful moment has arrived in which the flame of love has died out upon the altar. Unchastity of every description is love's sure destruction. . . . All theft is rendered impossible by true love for one's neighbor. Love sits as a sentinel at the portal of the lips, and arrests the faintest whisper of false witness against a neighbor; nay, rather dwells within the heart, and slays the thought that might have inspired the whisper. It is love and love alone that, finding satisfaction in God, satisfies the heart's hunger, and prevents all coveting."—G. Campbell Morgan, *The Ten Commandments* (New York: Fleming H. Revell Company, 1901), pp. 120, 121.

THE LAW MEASURES CHRISTIAN GROWTH.

One outstanding feature of God's laws often overlooked is that, although they set minimum boundaries, there are no maximum limits. For instance, we are not to kill or hate. But there is no limit to expressing God's kind of love.

What is new about Jesus' new commandment? John 13:34.

The new commandment was intended to enhance the Ten Commandments by a new and unique example of how they could be kept. Jesus came to give us a new understanding of the purpose, power, and promise of God's law, not only to show us how to live according to God's laws but also to provide the transforming grace that alone can enable us to surrender fully to God's will for us as it is expressed in His laws.

The Ten Commandments are not restrictions so much as they are word pictures of the kind of character God's children will reflect when they choose to live as He wants them to live. Compare the Ten Commandments in Exodus 20:3-17 with the positive expression of the principles of the Decalogue listed below:

1. *Loyalty*—God will be first. If we are Christ's we will long to bear His image and do His will.

2. *Worship*—We worship the unseen, not the seen. The things we once hated we now love.

3. *Reverence*—Our conversation, affections, and sympathies are in heaven. Our hearts are kept tender and subdued by the Spirit of Christ.

4. *Sanctification*—Christ is recognized as Creator and Re-Creator, not only by our keeping the seventh-day Sabbath but also in our full acceptance of the rest of redemption.

5. *Respect for Authority*—This begins in the home between parents and children, but extends to all relationships.

6. *Respect for Life*—In truly converted persons respect for our own life, as well as that of others, takes the place of anger, envy, and strife.

7. *Purity*—Passion, appetite, and will are brought into perfect submission to God.

8. *Honesty*—Integrity marks our relationships and the way we carry on business with our fellow humans and with God. Duty becomes a delight, and sacrifice a pleasure.

9. *Truthfulness*—When the heart is right our words and deeds will be true and right.

10. *Contentment*—The practice of holiness will be pleasant when there is perfect surrender to God. The joy of heaven will take the place of sadness and covetousness.

THE LAW IN THE NEW TESTAMENT.

What was Christ's attitude toward and relationship to the law? Matt. 5:17-19; John 14:15.

Christ fulfilled the moral law by living the principles of the law in His love for God and for humanity. He did not come to destroy the law. (See Matt. 5:17.) How could He destroy His love by loving? His entire life exemplified what God's love is like. It included being willing to go to the cross for the undeserving. When Jesus hung helpless on Calvary—lonely and hated—He accepted all the mockery, jeers, taunts, and rejection, gasping, "Father, forgive them." As He hung there, He gave the greatest demonstration of the law's eternal principles. Any idea that what happened on the cross changed the law comes from a superficial understanding of what took Jesus to the cross.

If there was any way that God could have saved the world and also spared His Son this utter disgrace and devastating anguish, He would have done it. But salvation's plan demands love for the undeserving. God went to the cross in an act of self-abandonment for others. This selfless act opens the true meaning of the law to our understanding.

The unchangeable principles that constitute the basis of God's nature are the basis of His government in heaven and on earth. Both Old and New Testaments reveal the inextricable union of God with His law.

Discover references to all the Ten Commandments in the New Testament by matching the texts in the column at the right with the Ten Commandments listed at the left:

_____ First commandment	a. Heb. 4:4-6
_____ Second commandment	b. Eph. 6:1-3
_____ Third commandment	c. 1 Thess. 1:9
_____ Fourth commandment	d. Matt. 5:21
_____ Fifth commandment	e. Matt. 5:27
_____ Sixth commandment	f. Acts 17:22-25
_____ Seventh commandment	g. Rom. 7:7
_____ Eighth commandment	h. Mark 10:19 (fourth in list)
_____ Ninth commandment	i. Matt. 5:33-37
_____ Tenth commandment	j. Rom. 13:9 (third in list)

As you measure your Christian development by the Ten Commandments as lived by Christ, in what specific areas do you need the Holy Spirit's help in order better to represent Christ's character to those about you?

A FAITH THAT WORKS.

Analyze Hebrews 11:6. What is the proper balance between faith and works?

Faith is absolutely essential. If it is missing, it will be impossible to please God, because we must not only believe in His existence but also must seek to please Him by allowing Him to transform our lives by His power.

How Enoch demonstrated faith (Heb. 11:5). Through Enoch, God proved to the world and to the universe what sinful, fallen human beings can achieve by God's grace through faith. By allowing God to work in Him, Enoch became "a light amid the moral darkness, a pattern man, a man who walked with God, being obedient to God's law—that law which Satan had refused to obey, which Adam had transgressed, which Abel obeyed, and because of his obedience, was murdered. And now God would demonstrate to the universe the falsity of Satan's charge that man cannot keep God's law. He would demonstrate that though man had sinned, he could so relate himself to God that he would have the mind and spirit of God and would be a representative symbol of Christ. This holy man was selected of God to denounce the wickedness of the world, and to evidence to the world that it is possible for men to keep all the law of God. . . .

"Enoch walked with God and 'had the testimony that his ways pleased God.' This is the privilege of every believer today."—Ellen G. White, *The Upward Look*, p. 228.

Faith works. The painting of the motto for a series of meetings was assigned to a local shop. The word *faith* was supposed to be placed on one side of the main theme and the word *works* on the other. Misunderstanding his instructions, the sign painter put these words at the center bottom portion of the banner so that it read, "Faith works." It made a most appropriate motto, for faith does not stand alone, isolated by itself. Wherever genuine faith is manifested, it is faith that works. (See Gal. 5:6.)

What does Galatians 2:17-21 tell us about how faith works?

Genuine "faith must reach a point where it will control the affections and impulses of the heart."—Ellen G. White, *Selected Messages*, book 1, p. 366. Have I allowed it to reach that point in my life?

THE RESULTS OF FAITH AT WORK.

Among the results of faith at work are the following:

1. Keeping the commandments and following God's will. Before Christ can come, God must demonstrate to the universe through His people that fallen humanity *can* keep His commandments by partaking of the divine nature as outlined in 2 Peter 1:3-11. (See Rom. 8:1-6.)

How does Revelation 14:12 summarize what the three angels' messages are about? (See lesson 12.)

Last-day commandment keepers are motivated by love. They love God so much that they are willing to do whatever He says, no matter what the consequences to themselves. They keep the faith of Jesus.

What attitude characterizes true commandment keeping? 1 John 5:3.

The keeping of God's law brings us the happiness and blessing that God intended His laws to bring to His people. Through disobedience we cheat ourselves of the blessings that harmony with God's laws brings. Not only did the Creator set in operation the laws that govern the regular movements of the heavenly bodies but He also instituted laws that regulate the life and health of the human beings He placed on this planet. These laws are intended to enhance rather than inhibit life. The "more abundant" life Jesus promised in John 10:10 to those who follow Him comes when by His grace we conform to the laws of life and health.

2. Heeding Christ's commission (Matt. 28:19, 20). Hearts filled with the love of God naturally will do everything possible to help save others. Commandment keepers do not have to be pushed into witnessing. It becomes their delight. We are eager to share with others.

The most effective way of teaching the truth is to make certain that through the power of the Holy Spirit we are obeying God's law to the best of our knowledge. Then, and only then, can we testify to the benefits of obedience to God's will. Obedience must be taught within the framework of a love response. We obey God because we love Him and appreciate what He has done and is doing for us.

FURTHER STUDY: "He who is trying to reach heaven by his own works in keeping the law, is attempting an impossibility. Man cannot be saved without obedience, but his works should not be of himself; Christ should work in him to will and to do of His good pleasure. If a man could save himself by his own works, he might have something in himself in which to rejoice. . . . All that man can do without Christ is polluted with selfishness and sin; but that which is wrought through faith is acceptable to God."—Ellen G. White, *Selected Messages*, book 1, p. 364.

"Do I wish to know by what kind of law God governs His people? Then I need only to read what the Scriptures reveal about the character of my Father, for His character is revealed in His law.

"Do I wish to know what kind of behavior will result if I live in obedience? Then I need to consider Christ Himself. His life was the law transmuted into a radiant, vibrant experience!

"Thus, as a Christian, I do not see the Ten Commandments as an expression of an arbitrary or a self-seeking will. Rather they are the revelation of the character of the heavenly Father, an expression of His gracious will for my happiness in the created order of things. In effect, He is saying 'This is the best and happiest way to live on Planet Earth.' "—Frank B. Holbrook, "What God's Law Means to Me," *Adventist Review*, Jan. 15, 1987, p. 16.

DISCUSSION QUESTIONS:

1. **Some people accuse Seventh-day Adventists of being "legalistic" and believing that they have to keep the commandments in order to be saved. How would you answer this question? How can you make the relationship between law and grace clear?**

2. **Do you understand that true lawkeeping is a love response to Jesus Christ? Do you understand that the Ten Commandments constitute God's character in words? Do you daily pray that the Commandments will become a part of your being? How would you describe the changes in your life after you accepted these principles?**

SUMMARY: God's remnant people believe in the perpetuity of the law of God. The law is the focal point of the great controversy between Christ and Satan. It is as eternal as God, being an expression of His character of love. Love to God and love to others make up the essence of the law. Salvation is all of grace and not of works, but its fruitage is obedience to the Commandments.

Lesson 19

The Sabbath

WHAT DOES THE BIBLE TEACH REGARDING THE SABBATH? How do we establish from Scripture that the seventh day of the week is the Sabbath that the Lord wishes us to observe? Why does He ask His believing people to keep the Sabbath day holy? Does the observance of the Sabbath have any bearing on our spiritual lives, or is it merely an option that God suggests because He knows that people would become over-tired if they worked seven days a week?

The Bible teaches that God's last-day seal is given to those who have entered into a special spiritual relationship with Christ. This relationship is the motivation and the power for obedience to all God's requirements, including Sabbath observance. In this sense, the Sabbath is the last-day seal of God.

Committed Christians want to do just what Jesus asks of them. They choose to observe the day He specifies, in the manner He specifies. What, then, does the Bible teach about the manner in which we should observe the Sabbath?

KEY THOUGHT. After six days of Creation, God instituted the Sabbath as a memorial of His creative work. The fourth commandment requires observance of the seventh-day Sabbath. Jesus and the apostles observed this day, teaching that it is a memorial of Creation and redemption and a special time for worship and communion with God.

> "Remember the sabbath day, to keep it holy. Six days shalt thou labour, and do all thy work: But the seventh day is the sabbath of the Lord thy God" (Exodus 20:8-10).

THE INSTITUTION OF THE SABBATH.

What were the three distinct acts by which God created the Sabbath? Gen 2:1-3.

1. _____

2. _____

3. _____

At the end of Creation week, after the world, its animal kingdom, and its two human inhabitants had come forth in absolute perfection from the Creator's hand, God brought the Sabbath into existence. Two institutions—marriage and the Sabbath—date back to Creation. Thus the Sabbath was known and observed prior to the giving of the law at Sinai. It is not a uniquely Jewish institution.

God did not rest at the end of Creation week because He was weary. (See Isa. 40:28.) Yet he "rested, and was refreshed" (Ex. 31:17). By blessing and sanctifying the Sabbath, God set it apart for a holy use. It became a day on which humankind in their original perfection would rest and enjoy special communion with their Creator.

Who was the Creator who rested on, blessed, and sanctified the Sabbath day? Col. 1:13-16; Heb. 1:1, 2.

Christ the Son, who created all things, certainly created the Sabbath. Therefore the Sabbath is a Christian institution. Christ did not give the Sabbath only to the Jews as a part of a temporary ceremonial system of laws. He instituted the Sabbath for all humanity for all time.

"Since the Sabbath is a memorial of the work of creation, it is a token of the love and power of Christ. The Sabbath calls our thoughts to nature, and brings us into communion with the Creator. In the song of the bird, the sighing of the trees, and the music of the sea, we still may hear His voice who talked with Adam in Eden in the cool of the day. And as we behold His power in nature we find comfort, for the word that created all things is that which speaks life to the soul."—Ellen G. White, *The Desire of Ages*, pp. 281, 282.

Do you sense your need of rest and refreshment on the day sanctified by the Creator? Of what special value to you can this day be?

THE SABBATH FROM CREATION TO SINAI.

Was the Sabbath observed by God's people before the giving of the law at Sinai? Gen. 26:5; Ex. 16:4, 5, 22-26.

Abraham's experience is presented in both the Old and New Testaments as a great example of righteousness by faith in Christ. (See Gen. 15:6; Romans 4; Gal. 3:6-14.) Yet Abraham obeyed God's laws. Sabbath observance was not a legalistic experience for him. It was a blessing because it was an act of faith in his Creator. (See Ellen G. White, *The Great Controversy*, p. 453.)

God reminded the Israelites of the Sabbath *before* He gave the Ten Commandments at Sinai. He commanded them to gather a double portion of manna on the sixth day in order to keep the seventh-day Sabbath holy. The period of slavery in Egypt had interrupted the practice of their religious observances. After the Exodus the Lord reintroduced the Sabbath.

What statement of Paul establishes that the giving of the Ten Commandments at Sinai was not the introduction of a system of righteousness by works? Gal. 3:15-18.

The covenant that God made with Abraham involved righteousness and salvation by faith. In effect the Lord told Abraham, "You believe in the Messiah to come, and I will give you forgiveness for the past, power for the present, and the assurance of eternal life." Paul taught that the giving of the law at Sinai did not annul the covenant given to Abraham. The Sabbath, which is at the very heart of the Ten Commandments, was not part of a works system. It was a vital part of righteousness-by-faith religion.

What kind of Sabbath observance does the fourth commandment stipulate? Ex. 20:8-11.

The fourth commandment gives a clear testimony as to why God commanded us to "remember the sabbath day." It forever establishes that Creation week consisted of seven 24-hour days. The Sabbath is a sign of the literal Creation week—"for in six days the Lord made heaven and earth" (Ex. 20:11). The seventh-day Sabbath is a bulwark against the error of the evolutionary theory, which teaches that life has evolved over long periods of time.

THE SABBATH IN ANCIENT ISRAEL.

In the days when Israel was a theocracy, what did the Lord command to be done to the Sabbath breaker? Ex. 31:14; Num. 15:30-36.

The individual who broke the Sabbath "presumptuously," or "with a high hand" (Num. 15:30, RSV), was to be cut off from Israel. Presumptuous sins were those committed in a proud spirit of rebellion against the Lord. (See Ex. 21:14, 15; Deut. 1:43; 17:12, 13.) In their wilderness experience, Israel had been specifically commanded by the Lord: "Ye shall kindle no fire throughout your habitations upon the sabbath day" (Ex. 35:3). In rebellion against this command, a man gathered wood for a fire on the Sabbath day. The Lord directed that he should be put to death.

Seventh-day Adventists are sometimes reminded that they do not put Sabbath breakers to death. This is said to be inconsistent because Adventists observe the Sabbath of the fourth commandment. We should notice, however, that the death penalty was to be meted out in Israel for rebellious breaking of any divine commandment, because Israel was a theocracy—ruled directly by God. (Compare Num. 15:30; Deut. 13:6-10; 21:18-21; 22:20-27.) No modern church puts to death members who are guilty of idolatry, immorality, disobedience to parents, or other sins of rebellion.

In view of Christ's glorious love made manifest at the cross, the New Testament makes continued willful disobedience extremely serious. (See Heb. 10:26-31.)

What is the special significance of the Sabbath to God's people? Ex. 31:13, 17; Eze. 20:12, 20; Heb. 4:9 (compare Isa. 56:1, 2, 6, 7; 58:13, 14).

Sanctification is holiness. Holiness, or righteousness, is God's gift to the one who has faith in Jesus Christ. (See Rom. 8:9, 10; compare Heb. 12:10.) Because the Sabbath is a sign of holiness, observance of the Sabbath is an inseparable part of the experience of righteousness and salvation by faith. Those who have received Christ's gift of holiness are willing to observe the Sabbath day; and by observing the Sabbath they are drawn into a closer fellowship of holiness with their Lord.

How do you think Sabbathkeeping can benefit your spiritual life?

44

CHRIST AND THE SABBATH.

What did Jesus do on the Sabbath day? Luke 4:16.

Why did Luke, writing years after Jesus' death, resurrection, and ascension, describe Jesus' Sabbath observance without commenting that such observance is no longer necessary for Christians? The answer is that Luke regarded Sabbath observance as part of God's plan, that involves living as Jesus did in obedience to God's commandments.

By what instruction did Jesus demonstrate His wish that His followers should observe the Sabbath after His death and resurrection? Matt. 24:20.

When "the abomination of desolation, spoken of by Daniel the prophet" is set up (Matt. 24:15), Jesus' people are to pray that their flight from their persecutors will not be on the Sabbath day. Jesus was referring to Daniel 8:13 and 9:27. The "abomination of desolation" (Matt. 24:15) was first set up when the Roman armies threatened Jerusalem (A.D. 66-70). The context indicates that a second fulfillment came in the Middle Ages. (See Matt. 24:15-29.) Because Matthew 24 is using historical events as a type of end-time events, we know that just prior to the Second Advent "the abomination of desolation" once more will become a threat to the religious liberty of God's people. The instruction of Matthew 24:20 applies as much to the end of time as it does to the first century and the Middle Ages. Therefore, the Lord intends His people to observe the Sabbath right down to His second advent. (See Ellen G. White, *The Great Controversy*, pp. 26, 36, 37.)

What do the following passages reveal regarding Jesus' method of Sabbath observance? Mark 2:23-28; 3:1-6.

Jesus taught that activities essential to maintain life, as well as healing and other activities designed to relieve suffering, are legitimate on the Sabbath. As Lord of the Sabbath, Jesus did not break the Sabbath command. He emphasized fellowship with God on the Sabbath day. But He did not rule out activities essential for such fellowship. (See also John 7:21-24; 9:1-16.)

THE APOSTLES AND THE SABBATH.

What action of Christ's followers after His death establishes that the seventh day of the week is the true Bible Sabbath? Luke 23:54–24:1, 7 (compare Mark 16:9; 1 Cor. 15:4).

Jesus died and was buried on the day of "preparation" for the Sabbath. The next day His followers rested "according to the commandment." Jesus rose from the dead the following day, the "first day of the week." Paul indicates that Christ's resurrection day was "the third day." The picture is clear. Jesus was crucified on Friday afternoon and rose on Sunday morning. The day between was the "sabbath day according to the commandment" (Luke 23:56). The true Bible Sabbath is the twenty-four hour period from sundown Friday until sundown Saturday. (See also Lev. 23:32; Neh. 13:19; Mark 1:21, 32.)

How many Sabbaths observed by the apostle Paul does the book of Acts record? What does this tell us about the attitude of the apostolic Christian church to Sabbath-keeping?

Acts 13:14, 15, 42-44 _____

Acts 16:12-15 _____

Acts 17:1, 2 _____

Acts 18:1, 4, 11 _____

These Sabbath meetings took place over a period of ten years, from about A.D. 45 to 55, well over a decade from the death of Jesus. Surely if there had been any inspired counsel to worship on another day, or not to worship on any day, Luke would have mentioned it.

In Philippi Paul and his associates kept the Sabbath "by a river side" (Acts 16:13). They did not go there because it was a convenient place to meet with Jews. It was a place "where prayer was wont to be made." The Greek may be translated: "where we thought (supposed, assumed) there was a place of prayer." The apostles looked for a quiet place to pray on the Sabbath day. The story establishes that the apostles observed the Sabbath as a day of spiritual rest, prayer, and witnessing. (Compare Heb. 4:4, 9.)

FURTHER STUDY: When John was a prisoner on the island of Patmos, on what day of the week did he receive a vision? Rev. 1:10; compare Mark 2:28.

John received his vision during the last decade of the first century A.D. It was not until the second half of the second century that some Christian writers used the Greek word for "Lord's day" to mean the first day of the week. They did this because Jesus rose from the dead on the first day of the week. Certain modern scholars have, therefore, assumed that the Lord's day on which John received his vision must have been Sunday.

Words and phrases often change meaning over a period of time. It is not valid reasoning to read a later meaning of a word or phrase into an earlier use of that word or phrase. We must consider John's understanding of the Lord's day in light of his background experiences. As one of the twelve disciples, he had heard Jesus' claim that He was "Lord" of the Sabbath (Mark 2:28). How natural it was for John to speak of the Sabbath as the Lord's day! The fact that John received a vision on a particular day does not sanctify that day. The Lord's day (the seventh-day Sabbath) had been sanctified 4,000 years earlier (Gen. 2:1-3).

DISCUSSION QUESTIONS:

1. How would you deduce from the passages that follow that God's last-day seal is given only to those who keep His Sabbath day holy? Rev. 7:1-3; 12:17; 14:1, 4-7; compare Rom. 4:11; Ex. 31:13; Heb. 8:10.

   "The fourth commandment alone of all the ten contains the seal of the great Lawgiver, the Creator of the heavens and the earth. Those who obey this commandment take upon themselves His name, and all the blessings it involves are theirs."—Ellen G. White, *Testimonies*, vol. 6, p. 350.

2. Why do none of the eight New Testament passages that mention the first day of the week speak of it as a day of worship? Matt. 28:1; Mark 16:2, 9; Luke 24:1; John 20:1, 19; Acts 20:7; 1 Cor. 16:1, 2.

SUMMARY: Because Christ established the Sabbath at Creation, it is a Christian institution. The Sabbath was intended for humanity in general. Jesus and the apostles kept the Sabbath, and Jesus instructed His followers to observe it until His second advent. Sabbathkeeping is a vital aspect of the spiritual experience of those who receive the end-time seal of God.

Lesson 20

Stewardship

CONSIDER YOUR WAYS. Seventeen years after Cyrus' decree ended the Babylonian captivity, the Jews who had returned to Jerusalem had become discouraged. Samaritan opposition to the building of the temple was fierce. When they neglected the work on the temple and turned to building their own homes, God challenged them: "Is it time for you yourselves to be living in your paneled houses, while this house remains a ruin?" (Hag. 1:4, NIV).

Twice in the first chapter of Haggai, God challenged the people to consider their ways. "Ye looked for much, and, lo, it came to little; and when ye brought it home, I did blow upon it" (Haggai 1:9). Why? Because in a time of great urgency for the work of the Lord they were caught up in a Laodicean-style sleeping sickness. (See Rev. 3:14-17.) What about us today? God challenges us to consider our ways, for nothing other than total commitment to Him is worthy in these last moments of time.

KEY THOUGHT: We are God's stewards, entrusted by Him with time, opportunities, abilities, possessions, and the blessings of the earth. We acknowledge God's ownership by faithful service to Him and our fellow men, by worshiping on the Sabbath, and by returning tithes and giving offerings for the proclamation of His gospel and the support and growth of His church.

> "Whatsoever ye do, do it heartily, as to the Lord, and not unto men; knowing that of the Lord ye shall receive the reward of the inheritance: for ye serve the Lord Christ" (Colossians 3:23, 24).

STEWARDSHIP RECOGNIZES GOD'S OWNERSHIP.

God has given us everything that love could provide. One loving gift is the power of choice. We alone decide how we will manage the gifts that love has given. In order to do so we must recognize that all we have and are comes from Him.

In what pointed language does God describe His ownership of the world? Ps. 50:10-12.

God wants *us*. Our sacrifices are of no value to Him except as they evidence our love for Him. It is as if a child receives a gift of money from his father and turns around to buy the father a "thank you" present with some of the money he has received. The father realizes that in the long run he paid for it himself, but he also realizes that he had given it to his son to use as he wished. The son's gift to him lets him know that his child loves him. The father also recognizes the value of encouraging a generous spirit in the boy.

What did David indicate about the ownership of all he and his people had? 1 Chron. 29:14.

"Men whom God has blessed with His bounties clasp their arms about their earthly treasure and make these bounties and blessings, which God has graciously given them, a curse by filling their hearts with selfishness and distrust of Him. They accept the goods lent them, yet claim them as their own, forgetting that the Master has any claim upon them, and refusing to yield to Him even the interest that He demands. . . . He has entrusted His treasure to stewards, that with them they may advance His cause and glorify His name."—Ellen G. White, *Testimonies*, vol. 2, p. 652.

What God seeks in return for all that He has given us is total commitment to Him. God's people in Hosea's day repudiated the Owner-manager concept. They did not acknowledge that their material blessings came from the Lord. (See Hosea 2:8.) The committed Christian will accept the fact that God is the owner of everything and that His children are the managers of these gifts. (See Matt. 6:25-34.) True peace of mind is the fruitage of understanding and practicing the principles of this Owner-manager relationship.

STEWARDSHIP IS TOTAL LIFE COMMITMENT.

Why do you think that Paul terms our commitment to God a "reasonable" service in Romans 12:1-3?

In the fullest sense stewardship can be defined as the complete and unreserved giving of ourselves to Jesus Christ. Our responsibility to God and to our fellow human beings does not depend on the quantity or quality of our material possessions. Our stewardship is based on two facts brought out in the texts that follow:

Isa. 44:24 _____

1 Cor. 6:20 _____

What basic principle is outlined in 1 Corinthians 10:31? How do our gifts to God reveal our love for Him? 2 Cor. 8:1-5.

If the church members in Macedonia had withheld their material and financial resources, it would have been proof that they had not given themselves fully to God. Notice the attitudes that characterized the Macedonian members when they gave to the glory of God.

"The troubles they have been through have tried them hard, yet in all this they have been so [1] exuberantly happy that from the depth of their poverty they have shown themselves [2] lavishly open-handed. [3] Going to the limit of their resources, as I can testify, and even beyond that limit, they [4] begged us most insistently, and on their own initiative, to be allowed to share in this generous service to their fellow-Christians" (2 Cor. 8:2-4, NEB).

"Nearly all the Macedonian believers were poor in this world's goods, but their hearts were overflowing with love for God and His truth, and they gladly gave for the support of the gospel. When general collections were taken up in the Gentile churches for the relief of the Jewish believers, the liberality of the converts in Macedonia was held up as an example to other churches. . . . It was not necessary to urge them to give; rather, they rejoiced in the privilege of denying themselves even of necessary things in order to supply the needs of others. When the apostle would have restrained them, they importuned him to accept their offering."—Ellen G. White, *The Acts of the Apostles*, pp. 343, 344.

STEWARDSHIP IS A PRIVILEGE.

When we love the Lord with our entire heart, mind, soul, and strength, we consider it a privilege to demonstrate our love in practical ways.

What is more important to God than our tithes and offerings? Matt. 23:23.

Stewardship, when understood as total life commitment, consists of much more than financial giving. In fact, material gifts make up only a small part of what those who choose to follow God are privileged to bring to Him. But what we do with the means He has provided us becomes a good indication of whether we are committed fully to Him.

If you place before you all your check stubs, cancelled checks, charge accounts, and receipts, you can see at a glance the direction of your life. As you survey all the material possessions of which you have made use—clothes, lands, homes, cars, bank accounts, stock certificates, food consumed, expenditure on entertainment, plus the tithes and offerings you have given—you can say, "There am I. That is the record of my life." Then ask yourself the question "Have I neglected the more important matters—justice, mercy, and faithfulness?"

Study the contrasting stories that follow. Indicate how they demonstrate the difference between total commitment and halfhearted service:

Acts 4:32–5:11—Ananias and Sapphira _____

_____

Mark 12:41-44—The widow's mite _____

_____

When Jesus said, "Where your treasure is, there will your heart be also" (Matt. 6:21), did He mean that our hearts follow where we put our treasure or that our treasure follows where we put our hearts? God's plan of stewardship focuses on the development of greater faith and stronger Christian characters. But we should not overlook the other side of the treasure-heart equation. Where our hearts are, our treasures naturally will follow. Ananias and Sapphira were not committed completely to Christ.

STEWARDSHIP BLESSES THE FAITHFUL STEWARD.

Not only do faithful stewards reap what they have sown, they actually receive from the Master's hands much more than they deserve. (See Matt. 25:21; John 10:10.)

What use is to be made of the tithe? Mal. 3:10-12; Lev. 27:30; 1 Cor. 9:13, 14.

What is the result of commitment to God's will and way? 2 Cor. 9:6-8.

Our giving demonstrates the extent and completeness of our commitment. It embraces all areas of our lives. The result of such giving is that grace abounds in and toward the giver. We reap what we sow.

In 2 Corinthians 9:7, the Greek word for "cheerful" is *hilaros* from which is derived our English word *hilarious*. It is interesting to note how solemn people's faces are when the offering plate passes by. There should be an enthusiastic, contagious joyfulness as we give to God not only our funds but also our entire beings.

How much does God expect us to give? Individuals can give only what God makes it possible for them to give; whether it be time, talents, money, or knowledge. Sharing the gospel is sharing what we are able to share—our spiritual experience and our relationship with God. We use the "gifts" of life in the process of sharing. Doing so not only blesses the recipients but also benefits those who give. As we learn to love by sharing, our characters are being molded in the image of the great Giver. Financial gifts are needed urgently in the cause of God. But lack of adequate funding is not, and never has been, the basic problem that has hindered the development of God's work through the centuries. The great need has been the development of a truly spiritual experience in the recipients of God's gift of life.

Apply Hebrews 12:2, "Looking unto Jesus the author and finisher of our faith; who for the joy that was set before him endured the cross," to your experience. What do you anticipate will be the result of entering into a full, complete, and happy partnership with Jesus?

As far as stewardship is concerned, what special meaning can be found in Christ's fifth beatitude recorded in Matthew 5:7?

More than the spirit of mercy or forgiveness is intended here. When Christ dwells in our hearts fully, they will overflow with His benevolence. We are inspired to share the blessings received with those about us. Thus begins a chain reaction of mercy and benevolence that is God's means of developing Christlike children to fill His kingdom. The more we give, the more we gain in return.

A healing power. "If the mind is free and happy, from a consciousness of rightdoing and a sense of satisfaction in causing happiness to others, it creates a cheerfulness that will react upon the whole system, causing a freer circulation of the blood and the toning up of the entire body. The blessing of God is a healing power, and those who are abundant in benefiting others will realize that wondrous blessing in both heart and life."—Ellen G. White, *Counsels on Health*, p. 28.

What aspects of giving in the early church are illustrated in the passages that follow?

Rom. 15:26, 27 _____

1 Cor. 9:9-14 _____

True stewardship should never be confused with righteousness by works. It is built on a confident, loving relationship with our Lord. If we love the Lord, we will share that love in many practical ways with those about us. We will do so spontaneously, perhaps not even realizing what we are doing. (See Matt. 25:34-40.) In turn we will discover that we have gained all through giving all, in this life, as well as eternally.

The basis of all stewardship is the life and death of our Lord Jesus Christ. Stewardship is utter selflessness. It is giving oneself completely to God, as well as giving ourselves freely in service to fellow human beings.

When we see the simple life that Jesus lived and the horrible death that He died, how can we withhold that which He asks of us? Christ gave not merely what He had; He gave Himself. Can we give anything less? (See 2 Cor. 8:9.)

FURTHER STUDY: The Adventist practice of returning tithes and offerings follows the principles outlined in Scripture. Review in your mind God's program of motivating stewardship on the basis of love for the Lord.

Study the book of Haggai, noting how the people had neglected God's work, putting their priority on selfish goals. Note the interesting way God used to let them know that they were hurting themselves by their selfishness. Then concentrate on discovering the blessings that followed their recognition of their neglect and their enthusiastic commitment to the work of rebuilding the temple. What lessons can we learn from their experience?

DISCUSSION QUESTIONS:

1. In your personal experience, how have you found that God blesses you when you commit to Him your entire self and all He has given you?

2. On the question of tithing, many testify that nine-tenths of their income goes much farther with God's blessing than ten-tenths without it. Are you willing to accept God's challenge to put Him to the test on this point?

3. Have you as yet experienced the peace that results from acknowledging God's ownership of all you possess? Do you trust God enough to surrender your time, talents, treasure, and body temple for His service and the blessing of your fellow human beings?

SUMMARY: The Bible teaches that stewardship begins with our recognition that all we have comes from God. Stewardship is a great blessing, a privilege given to us by God for nurture in love and for gaining the victory over selfishness and covetousness. We also rejoice in the blessings that come to others as a result of God's abundant love bestowed so freely on us that we are privileged to share with those in need.

Lesson 21

Christian Behavior

WHY DO WE HAVE STANDARDS OF BEHAVIOR? Many Christians of various denominations are increasingly concerned about the need for standards in their churches. As they compare the moral and ethical decline in most societies with the manner of life that God approves, they become more and more conscious that the churches have a responsibility to teach Christian standards of behavior.

Moreover, Christian believers who view themselves as temples of the Holy Spirit search for more healthful ways of eating and drinking, as well as for beneficial exercise, recreation, and rest.

How is Christian behavior related to the gospel? First, we must understand that the cross reveals the utter uselessness of trying to earn merit through a particular lifestyle. Standards do not save; they demonstrate the saving presence of Christ in the heart.

Second, trying to be different in the way we look, act, and think merely for the sake of being different from the world is irrational. There are reasons for every standard the church upholds. Jesus was different, not for the sake of difference, but because He conformed to the divine principles for vibrant, abundant, healthful living.

KEY THOUGHT. For Christians, the life of Jesus is the example. We wish to practice health habits and modes of dress, adornment, and entertainment that are thoroughly consistent with the character and instruction of our Lord.

"I came that they may have life, and have it abundantly" (John 10:10, RSV).

THE MORE ABUNDANT LIFE.

What kind of life did Moses set before Israel? Deut. 30:11-16; 28:1, 2.

God promised ancient Israelites health, happiness, and prosperity if they obeyed His commandments. That meant practicing the ethical and moral principles given through Moses—the Ten Commandments and the laws applying these commands to the life situation of the people. The Ten Commandments are also the basis of Christian standards. (See Rom. 3:31; 7:7.) The righteous principles of these laws will be fulfilled in the lives of true believers. (See Rom. 8:3, 4.)

Whose ownership are we urged to acknowledge? What is the basis of this ownership? 1 Cor. 6:19, 20.

We all know by experience that rules listed in an operation manual for various types of equipment—automobiles, furnaces, microwaves, et cetera—are designed to give the owner the best possible service. So it is with life. God, the Owner and Proprietor, desires our best good. He alone knows what will provide us the maximum amount of happiness. Why do some people rebel against standards of dress, diet, and recreation? (See Rom. 8:6-8.)

"To set the mind on the things of the Spirit, and to have the thoughts and desires governed solely by the Spirit of God, result in that healthful, life-giving harmony of all the functions of the soul that is a sure pledge and foretaste of the life to come."—*SDA Bible Commentary*, vol. 6, p. 563.

The presence of the Holy Spirit brings love, joy, and peace into the life. (See Gal. 5:22.) The Spirit within is the kingdom of God within. The trusting Christian enjoys "righteousness, and peace, and joy in the Holy Ghost" (Rom. 14:17).

What has Christ done for us that gives Him the right to direct our way of life? Col. 1:13-17; 1 Pet. 1:15-19.

What greater claim could Christ have upon us than that He created us and, when we fell into sin, died to buy us back from the dominion of the evil one? Are these not sufficient reasons for Him to direct our conduct?

THE CHRISTIAN'S HEALTH.

Because God cares for us, He has given us information for the maintenance of our bodies. In Scripture there are more than one thousand texts that deal with a person's physical health. In addition, God has graciously given us specific details as to the best way to care for our bodies. Books such as Ellen White's *The Ministry of Healing, Counsels on Health, and Counsels on Diet and Foods* are indispensable to those who really seek to know God's will in these matters.

What health instruction do you find in these passages?

Gen. 1:29; 3:18 _____

Lev. 11:1-20 _____

Prov. 20:1; 23:29-32 _____

Isa. 65:3, 4; 66:15-17 _____

God originally gave to mankind a vegetarian diet. Even after the Fall, they were to eat the produce of the field. Because plant life had been destroyed by the Flood, survival demanded an alternative food supply. After the Flood, Noah and his family were permitted to eat flesh food, but specifically commanded not to eat blood. (See Gen. 9:3, 4.) The command against eating blood had both health and symbolic significance. Later the Lord commanded Israel: "It shall be a perpetual statute throughout your generations in all your dwelling places, that you eat neither fat nor blood" (Lev. 3:17, RSV; compare 7:26, 27). God explained: "For the life of the flesh is in the blood; and I have given it for you upon the altar to make atonement for your souls" (Lev. 17:11, RSV). Not only is disease transmitted through blood, but blood is an animal's life, symbolizing the life of Christ shed for our sins.

Through Moses, the Lord gave instruction as to which animals should be used as food and which should not. Those animals that both chew the cud and are cloven-footed could be eaten. The swine was considered the most unclean and was strictly forbidden. Fish must have fins and scales, and certain birds were forbidden. Alcoholic beverages were forbidden. (See Samuele Bacchiocchi, *Wine in the Bible* [Berrien Springs, Michigan: Biblical Perspectives], 1989.)

These health principles are timeless; Jesus and His disciples observed them.

Why does the Seventh-day Adventist Church recommend a vegetarian diet to its members? What are the disadvantages of a flesh-food diet?

"There needs to be presented to all students and physicians, and by them to others, that the whole animal creation is more or less diseased. Diseased meat is not rare, but common. Every phase of disease is brought into the human system through subsisting upon the flesh of dead animals. The feebleness and weakness in consequence of a change from a meat diet will soon be overcome, and physicians ought to understand that they should not make the stimulus of meat eating essential for health and strength. All who leave it alone intelligently, after becoming accustomed to the change, will have health of sinews and muscles."—Ellen G. White, *Counsels on Diet and Foods*, p. 292.

The cholesterol content of flesh foods is high. Cholesterol is one of the main causes of arteriosclerosis (hardening of the arteries) that produces heart disease.

Why is the use of alcohol, tobacco, and the misuse of other drugs alien to Christian lifestyle? Dan. 1:8-21.

1. Alcohol causes the loss of mental and physical control. It is one of the main causes of tragedy on the highways. It is estimated that more than 10 percent of all admissions to public mental institutions are the result of chronic alcoholism. Alcohol damages the highest centers of the brain; those concerned with behavior, speech, and memory. Concentrated doses damage the nervous system.

2. The dangers of smoking to health have been heavily documented in recent years. Lung cancer, pulmonary emphysema, and heart disease are common among smokers. In 1875 Ellen G. White wrote: "Tobacco is a slow, insidious poison, and its effects are more difficult to cleanse from the system than those of liquor."—Ellen G. White, *Temperance*, p. 55.

3. The Bible condemns misuse of drugs. The "sorcerers" (Rev. 21:8; 22:15; Greek *pharmakoi*) are "mixers of poisons," or "poisoners." Such people in ancient times were often involved in occult practices. At the coming of Jesus, people who misuse drugs will be classed among murderers, adulterers, and idolaters. Not only the more potent drugs but also those contained in tea and coffee are harmful to health.

DRESS AND ADORNMENT.

What principles designed to direct the way we dress are spelled out in the Bible?

1 Tim. 2:9, 10 _____

1 Pet. 3:3-5 _____

God wants the character of each believer "to be conformed to the image of his Son" (Rom. 8:29). The Holy Spirit brings the Christian progressively nearer to the image of Christ (2 Cor. 3:18). If Christ is living out His life through individuals (Gal. 2:20), then they will follow the pattern of dress and conduct that Christ respects.

What is that pattern? Although women are mentioned in Scripture when dress is discussed, the counsel equally applies to men. The modes of dress that the Bible condemns are: (1) extravagant hairstyles; (2) wearing of gold; (3) wearing of pearls; (4) costly attire. (See 1 Tim. 2:9, 10.) In context, it is obvious that Paul is referring to extravagant hairdos and clothes. Obviously a disorderly and unkempt appearance is just as likely to attract attention to oneself and so to break the Bible principle.

The mode of dress that the Bible approves is: (1) respectable; (2) modest; (3) moderate, showing good judgment and self-control; (4) such as reveals reverence for God; (5) such as demonstrates a pure, humble heart.

The secret of dressing properly is found in Philippians 2:5 and Hebrews 12:2. If we have the mind of Christ, focusing our eyes on Him rather than on self, the dress, makeup, and jewelry problem will certainly disappear. We will harbor no desire to attract attention to ourselves, but will always want to reflect the humble character of Jesus. The Scriptures distinguish clearly between the fashions of the world and those that honor God. (Compare Rev. 12:1 and 17:4, 5.) The description of the woman who represents the true church includes modesty, purity, and beauty. By contrast, the woman representing Babylon is extravagantly adorned. Those who enjoy fellowship with Christ can easily detect the difference.

Ask yourself, How would Jesus dress in the circumstances in which I find myself? Of course, we do not know exactly how Jesus dressed under all circumstances. But we can allow ourselves to be guided by the pure and righteous principles that governed everything Jesus did.

ENTERTAINMENT THAT CHRIST APPROVES.

To what extent does God wish to direct our thoughts? 2 Cor. 10:4, 5. What effect do our thoughts have on our words and actions? Matt. 15:18-20.

Because the Lord wants us to allow the Holy Spirit to control our thoughts, no form of entertainment that directs our minds in evil channels is consistent with Christian principle. Evil thoughts precede evil words and deeds. Therefore, what we read and see, whether in the privacy of our homes or in public places of entertainment, has enormous significance for the way we speak and act. To allow evil demons to control our thoughts is to reject the protective control of the Holy Spirit.

What will the believer do when he or she sees evil? What promise is given to such a person? Isa. 33:15-17.

A person's control center is the mind. We must keep our mind receptors keen and clean. The major purpose for the Christian health program is to keep the mind alert to the wiles of Satan and strong to resist him. The mind is to be the dwelling place of the Spirit of Christ.

The nondrug-taking, nonalcohol-drinking, nonsmoking vegetarian who exercises and rests well is just as vulnerable as those who do not follow such a lifestyle if his or her television viewing is out of control. Television is one of Satan's most deadly weapons against Christians today. Programs filled with violence, immorality, and dishonesty destroy moral and ethical values.

What blessings does God promise the person who turns away from the sinful pleasures of the world and centers his or her life wholly in Christ? 1 John 2:15-17; Col. 3:1-4.

Committed Christians do not ask what is wrong with this or that kind of entertainment; they ask, Can I retain the controlling presence of the Holy Spirit over my mind while engaging in this pleasure? Can I maintain my fellowship with Jesus while indulging in this kind of entertainment? (See Phil. 4:8.)

Applying the Bible principles to your life, do you see any practices you need to change? How can you make these changes?

FURTHER STUDY: Think positively about the joy of exercising your spiritual gifts in service for others. How can this benefit your health? See 1 Corinthians 12 and 13. Read Ellen G. White's *Counsels on Health*, pp. 19-25; *Testimonies*, vol. 4, pp. 628-648, 652, 653.

God has greatly blessed Adventists in giving them a total life concept. We are happy, not because we are better than others, but because the Lord has shown us the relationship between spiritual, mental, and physical health. We invite you to make the commitment to live as Christ lived.

"Christians must be like Christ. They should have the same spirit, exert the same influence, and have the same moral excellence that He possessed. The idolatrous and corrupt in heart must repent and turn to God. Those who are proud and self-righteous must abase self and become penitent and meek and lowly in heart. The worldly-minded must have the tendrils of the heart removed from the rubbish of the world, around which they are clinging, and entwined about God; they must become spiritually minded."—*Testimonies*, vol. 5, pp. 249, 250.

DISCUSSION QUESTIONS:

1. **You sincerely wish to serve Christ faithfully, but you cannot tear yourself away from spiritually damaging television programs. After thinking and praying about the problem, what do you consider to be the solution?**

2. **How can a person overcome the habit of eating and drinking in an unhealthful way? Is knowledge of what is healthful sufficient?**

3. **We have discovered that the basic principle governing what should entertain us is purity of thought. What practical applications of this principle can we make in regard to what we read and view?**

4. **To what extent do you think there is room for cultural differences in the manner in which it is appropriate for Christians to dress?**

SUMMARY: The Bible teaches that the power of the indwelling Christ enables the believer to live in harmony with Bible principles in regard to health, dress, and entertainment. Correct behavior does not earn our salvation; it results from the saving power of Jesus in the heart.

Lesson 22

Marriage and the Family

CHRIST BRINGS HAPPINESS TO FAMILIES. Aspirin does not cure toothaches. It merely treats the symptoms. A tragically large number of homes and families are unhappy ones. But much of what is being done to help solve this problem merely treats the symptoms rather than the disease. We will not find long-lasting cures for home problems until we get down to the basic cause—selfishness and sin. Only the Great Physician has the miracle cure for human unhappiness. Happy homes depend on Christ dwelling in the hearts of the occupants.

All of us, whether married or not, are members of a family of one kind or another. All of us need Christ's help in order to improve our relationships. In Christ we also can find relief from such related problems as loneliness, stress, anger, and insensitivity.

A happy, healthy, well-functioning family provides in turn a climate that fosters a better relationship with our Lord and a stronger witness to the community around us.

KEY THOUGHT: Marriage was divinely established in Eden and affirmed by Jesus to be a lifelong union between a man and a woman in loving companionship. Mutual love, honor, respect, and responsibility are the fabric of this relationship, which is to reflect the closeness and permanence of the relationship between Christ and His church. Increasing family closeness is one of the marks of the final gospel message.

"My little children, let us not love in word, neither in tongue; but in deed and in truth" (1 John 3:18).

HAPPY FAMILIES.

As the "Prince of Peace" (Isa. 9:6), Jesus brings peace to all who commit themselves to Him. Jesus never needlessly wounded anyone. The Lord looked upon His disciples and followers as His family. (See Matt. 12:50; John 15:15.) Notice how carefully He treated Judas and sought to win His affection. In John 13:1 we read that Jesus "having loved his own which were in the world . . . loved them unto the end." When we follow His example the peace He promised (John 14:27) will make our relationships happy ones.

Notice specifically the counsel the apostle gives husbands and wives in 1 Peter 3:7. What does Peter set forth as the ideal in Christian relationships? Verses 8-11.

"Too many cares and burdens are brought into our families, and too little of natural simplicity and peace and happiness is cherished. There should be less care for what the outside world will say and more thoughtful attention to members of the family circle. There should be less display and affectation of worldly politeness, and much more tenderness and love, cheerfulness and Christian courtesy, among the members of the household. Many need to learn how to make home attractive, a place of enjoyment. Thankful hearts and kind looks are more valuable than wealth or luxury, and contentment with simple things will make home happy if love be there."—Ellen G. White, *The Adventist Home*, p. 108.

In what way are we responsible for the happiness and well-being of the members of our church family? James 1:27; 1 John 4:11, 12.

In the same way that the spokes of the wheel come closer to one another as they approach the hub, our church and family relationships will come closer together as we come closer to Christ. It is part of "pure religion" to give special attention to the needs of the members of our church family (James 1:27; Isa. 1:17). For some, the church provides the only family they have. The Lord calls us to love one another (1 John 4:7, 20, 21).

Am I living so close to Jesus that He can use me and direct me to minister to the special needs of those in my church family who require my attention and assistance?

MARRIAGE ESTABLISHED BY GOD.

When God brought the animals to Adam for naming, the first man soon discovered that they came in pairs, yet he was alone. Because of the lonely man's need for companionship, God created Eve. (See Gen. 2:18.) When Adam saw her, he recognized that she would meet his needs, and he felt a deep responsibility to meet hers. The first marriage, celebrated by God in Eden, was to be a model for marriages in succeeding generations.

How did Christ honor the institution of marriage when He lived on earth? John 2:1-11.

"No shadow of worldly levity marred . . . [Jesus'] conduct; yet He found pleasure in scenes of innocent happiness, and by His presence sanctioned the social gathering. A Jewish marriage was an impressive occasion, and its joy was not displeasing to the Son of man. By attending this feast, Jesus honored marriage as a divine institution."—Ellen G. White, *The Desire of Ages*, p. 151.

In the light of the symbol of the new wine as the presentation of the gospel in Mark 2:22, how does this symbol relate to the place of the gospel in the marriage relationship? "Like every other one of God's good gifts entrusted to the keeping of humanity, marriage has been perverted by sin; but it is the purpose of the gospel to restore its purity and beauty."—Ellen G. White, *Thoughts From the Mount of Blessing*, p. 64.

How did God's plan provide for equality in the husband-wife relationship while maintaining the gospel principle of mutual submission and service? Eph. 5:21-33.

In Ephesians 5 the husband-wife relationship is compared to that of Christ to His church, which places marriage on a solid, Christ-centered foundation. In this chapter we discover a concept of marriage that seems to be largely lost in our time. If Paul's counsel were heeded, divorce virtually would be eliminated. Even young Christian couples who have the best intentions in the world often view marriage as a private transaction between themselves. Their center of focus is on the great love they have for each other. However, if marriage is to be successful, it must focus on another—Jesus. This most intimate of personal relationships involves a love that is greater than all human love—a love understood in the light of the cross.

A LIFELONG UNION.

When Paul compared the husband-wife relationship to that of Christ and the church, he established a model that indicates that the relationship is to last for the rest of the partners' lives. The peace and joy of heaven enable those united in Christ to weather the storms and trials of life. God's covenant love knits together what sin separates. (See Col. 2:2.) The everlasting covenant, with the cross of Christ at its center, helps bind men and women closer to each other in the marriage union. Even when spouses become alienated, the cross of Christ can break down the hostility. (See Eph. 2:13, 14.)

Children can sense whether mother and father love each other. While one father was on a temporary assignment in an area far from home, he and his family lived in a small hotel room. Owing to lack of play space in the room, his little girl was playing "house" in the hotel lobby. One of the other guests in the hotel said to the little girl, "It's a shame that you don't have a home of your own to play in." Quick as a wink the girl responded, "Oh, we *do* have a home. We just don't have a house to put it in here." She recognized that love made a home out of a hotel room.

How does Christ express the seriousness and moral consequences of divorce? Matt. 5:31, 32; 19:3-9; Luke 16:18. What counsel does Paul give on the question of divorce? 1 Cor. 7:10, 11.

There are home and family situations that are far from the ideal that make this question of divorce one for which there are no simple answers. Yet consider the spiritual implications of divorce. It is the severing of relationships between persons whom God has joined together. It involves breaking not only vows made to another person but vows made to God. Even in a civil ceremony in a registry office, where vows are not made to God, promises are made mutually that are sacred. Paul's burden seems to be that everything should be done that can be done to hold a marriage together. But a marriage partner should not remain in a situation that threatens his or her life.

How can the forgiveness of God become a motivating factor in my life and family relationships? How can it help me forgive myself as well as others? What can we do as church members to help others deal with the guilt, anger, fear, and grief that arise from difficult marriages?

PARENTS AND CHILDREN.

Parents assume a solemn responsibility when they have children. Children are a precious gift of God. They are younger members of the Lord's family to be loved and led to Him. The parents' first responsibility is to live consecrated Christian lives before their children.

What specific role is delegated to fathers? Eph. 6:4.

The father's place in the life and training of the child is significant. Passages such as Deuteronomy 6:1-9 picture the father providing for, training, and correcting his children in a way that they may know and understand the commandments of God. The father is to serve as the priest of the home. In the absence of a Christian father this responsibility falls upon the mother.

"All members of the family center in the father. He is the lawmaker, illustrating in his own manly bearing the sterner virtues: energy, integrity, honesty, patience, courage, diligence, and practical usefulness. The father is in one sense the priest of the household, laying upon the altar of God the morning and evening sacrifice."—Ellen G. White, *The Adventist Home*, p. 212.

What qualities characterize a mother whose husband and children call her "blessed"? Prov. 31:10-28.

"The tenderest earthly tie is that between the mother and her child. The child is more readily impressed by the life and example of the mother than by that of the father, for a stronger and more tender bond of union unites them.

"The thoughts and feelings of the mother will have a powerful influence upon the legacy she gives her child. . . . A Christian mother will ever be wide awake to discern the dangers that surround her children. She will keep her own soul in a pure, holy atmosphere."—Ellen G. White, *The Adventist Home*, pp. 240, 241.

What is the responsibility of children toward their parents? Ex. 20:12; Eph. 6:1-3.

In the light of James 1:27, in what practical ways should I as a church member respond to the needs of single parents and their children in my church?

INCREASING FAMILY CLOSENESS.

Happiness is the product of Christlike, other-centered living. The family that prays and plays together stays together. "Hearts that are filled with the love of Christ can never get very far apart."—Ellen G. White, *Testimonies*, vol. 5, p. 335. Families that attend church and work together for others find joy and happiness.

What keys to successful family relationships are found in the passages that follow?

Matt. 5:44 _____

Matt. 7:1-5 _____

Rom. 12:10 _____

Eph. 4:32 _____

The critical point in a marriage. "As life with its burden of perplexity and care meets the newly wedded pair, the romance with which imagination so often invests marriage disappears. Husband and wife learn each other's character as it was impossible to learn it in their previous association. This is a most critical period in their experience. The happiness and usefulness of their whole future life depend upon their taking a right course now. Often they discern in each other unsuspected weaknesses and defects; but the hearts that love has united will discern excellencies also heretofore unknown. Let all seek to discover the excellencies rather than the defects. Often it is our own attitude, the atmosphere that surrounds ourselves, which determines what will be revealed to us in another."—Ellen G. White, *The Ministry of Healing*, p. 360.

If you strike a single key on the piano, the sound you get is not harmony. In order to get harmony you must have at least one other note. It may be one close by or one at some distance, but if it is a harmonious note it will blend until the two sound like one but produce a more beautiful tone than would either if struck separately or if one were played twice as loud.

What benefits come to the family through the practice of regular family worship? What can I do to help family worship deepen the individual spiritual experience of the members of my family? What other spiritual activities will bring us closer to each other and to the Lord?

FURTHER STUDY: How can the principle of leaving father and mother (Gen. 2:24) be balanced with honoring father and mother (Ex. 20:12)? What do the words *leave* and *honor* mean? What restriction did God place on marriage in order to preserve the sanctity of the home? 2 Cor. 6:14.

DISCUSSION QUESTIONS:

1. **What can be done to share the blessings of a happy home with neighboring families? One suggestion is to invite them to enjoy an evening worship with your family. If possible sing several hymns, ask the children to participate in reading passages of Scripture, share a Bible story or two, then have prayer together. Make your guests feel welcome and comfortable. Be sensitive as to whether or not they are willing to participate in the worship.**

2. **Do I realize that a happy marriage relationship and home do not come by accident, but are a result of specific planning and working the plan?**
   - **If I am single and have plans for marriage or am thinking of marriage, am I making a deliberate effort to ensure that my plans have God's approval?**
   - **If there is a problem in my marriage relationship, am I doing everything possible through my own commitment to Christ to bring about healing?**
   - **In what way has Christ's presence brought happiness and joy to me? How can I share what I have learned with other family members this week?**

SUMMARY: Part of the Elijah message of Malachi 4 reads, "He will turn the hearts of the fathers to their children, and the hearts of the children to their fathers" (Mal. 4:6, NIV). This has special application to God's remnant people in the end-time. A Christian home, where the love of Christ reigns supreme, is a powerful witness to the effectiveness of the gospel of Jesus Christ.

Christ's Heavenly Ministry

CHRIST MINISTERS IN THE HEAVENLY SANCTUARY.
God designed the ancient Israelite sanctuary and its services to point forward to and explain the sacrifice, heavenly mediation, and judgment ministry of the Lord Jesus Christ. The sacrifices offered in the sanctuary court pointed forward to the cross. The priestly work in the holy place represented Christ's intercessory ministry after His resurrection. The high priest's work in the Most Holy Place symbolized Christ's final ministry of vindication in the pre-advent, investigative judgment.

Why is there need for an end-time, pre-advent judgment? God is concerned that the angels and the inhabitants of the unfallen universe should be thoroughly convinced that the people He saves have a right to be in heaven. Moreover, God wants His earthly people to have victory over sin. By faith, the character of Jesus is to become ours. The judgment reveals who has received His character and who has refused it. He cannot take to heaven people who refuse to receive the Holy Spirit as the power to overcome sin.

KEY THOUGHT. After His resurrection, Jesus ascended to the heavenly sanctuary, where He mediates for repentant sinners. After 1844 the pre-advent judgment decides whose names God can retain in the book of life for eternity.

"He who conquers shall be clad thus in white garments, and I will not blot his name out of the book of life; I will confess his name before my Father and before his angels" (Revelation 3:5, RSV).

THE ANCIENT ISRAELITE SANCTUARY.

When the children of Israel were traveling from Egypt to the Promised Land, the Lord commanded Moses to build a sanctuary that would be His dwelling place, as well as a place of worship for the people. (See Ex. 25:8.) This sanctuary was not the same as a modern church. It consisted of a courtyard that housed a tent or tabernacle. The tent contained two rooms, one twice the size of the other.

Describe the two items of furniture in the court of the sanctuary. Ex. 27:1-8; 30:17-21. Briefly describe the contents of the holy place. Ex. 25:23-32; 30:1-8.

Describe the contents of the Most Holy Place. Ex. 25:10-21.

The two items of furniture in the court were the altar of burnt offering and the laver. The Holy Place contained a candlestick with seven branches (*menorah*), the table of shewbread, and the altar of incense. In the Most Holy Place was the ark of the covenant containing the tables of stone, on which were written the Ten Commandments. The ark was a symbol of the throne of God. The presence of the Lord was manifested above the mercy seat, the cover of the ark. (See Num. 7:89; 1 Sam. 4:4; 2 Kings 19:15.)

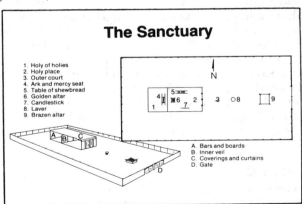

The court was the place for animal sacrifices. The ministry in the Holy Place represented priestly intercession or mediation. God dwelt in the Most Holy Place, where each year on the Day of Atonement the judgment took place. Sacrifice, mediation, and judgment are the three great ministries Jesus provided to save the believing worshiper.

CHRIST—DEITY, SACRIFICE, AND HIGH PRIEST.

Who accompanied Israel in their travels, dwelling upon the throne in the Most Holy Place of the sanctuary? 1 Cor. 10:1-4; Ex. 40:33-38.

The Greek word translated "followed" in 1 Corinthians 10:4 may also mean "accompanied." Christ accompanied Israel in their wilderness travels. He was in the pillar of cloud by day and the pillar of fire by night. When the sanctuary was stationary, Christ occupied the throne in the Most Holy Place. (See *Christ's Object Lessons*, p. 288.)

Whose sacrifice was represented by every animal sacrifice offered in the court of the sanctuary? John 1:29; Heb. 10:1-12. What was symbolized by the daily ministry of the priests in the court and the Holy Place? Heb. 4:14-16; 7:23-28; 8:1, 2.

Atonement for sin was provided when: (1) the repentant one placed his hand on the head of an animal sacrifice and confessed his sin (Lev. 4:29 first part); (2) he took the life of the animal (Lev. 4:29 last part); (3) the priest sprinkled the blood either on the horns of the altar of burnt offering (for the ruler or common person), or in the holy place before the veil and on the horns of the altar of incense (for a priest or the entire congregation). (See Lev. 4:6, 7, 17, 18, 25, 30.) Thus, "atonement" included priestly ministry (sprinkling of blood) after the sacrifice. The priests cooked and ate part of the flesh of the sin-offering for the average person and the ruler (Lev. 6:26, 29, 30). This represented the priest taking upon himself the sin of the penitent sinner. (See Lev. 10:16-18.) Because the priest later ministered in the holy place, the sin was taken into the presence of God and symbolically transferred to the sanctuary. In the case of the sin-offering for the priest and the entire congregation, the officiating priests ate none of the sacrifice.

The sprinkling of the blood and the eating of the flesh by the priests symbolized that the demands of the broken law had been met, that the sinner had been relieved of guilt, and that the sanctuary now contained a *pardoned* record. Christ bore our sins on the cross (1 Peter 2:24). Now in the heavenly sanctuary He applies the merits of His shed blood, and repentant sinners are forgiven. (See Heb. 9:12-14; Ellen G. White, *The Great Controversy*, p. 489.)

THE PRE-ADVENT INVESTIGATIVE JUDGMENT.

In the earthly sanctuary, what were the most important events of the Day of Atonement? Lev. 16:6-10, 15-22.

What was the purpose of the high priest's ministry in the Most Holy Place? Lev. 16:29, 30, 33.

Of the two goats taken by the high priest on the Day of Atonement, one represented Christ and the other represented Satan. The animal representing Christ was slain, symbolizing Christ's death upon the cross. The high priest sprinkled some of its blood on the mercy seat in the Most Holy Place, on the altar of incense in the holy place, and on the altar of burnt offering in the court. Thus every part of the sanctuary was symbolically cleansed of the record of pardoned sin. The sins of the people, who had brought their sin offerings during the year, had been forgiven already. (See Lev. 4:26, 31, 35). By the sprinkling of blood in the daily service the "pardoned" record had been symbolically retained in the sanctuary. It was necessary to cleanse the sanctuary of this record of pardoned sin on the Day of Atonement.

While the high priest was ministering in the Most Holy Place, the people in the court were examining their hearts to be sure that all their sins had been confessed and put away. The Day of Atonement was an annual judgment day, on which the sanctuary, priests, and people were cleansed.

After the vision of the "little horn" power persecuting God's people for centuries, what scene was Daniel shown? Dan. 7:8-10, 13, 14, 21, 22, 25, 26.

The heavenly pre-advent judgment is the antitype of the Israelite Day of Atonement. The period of papal supremacy ended in 1798 when Napoleon's general took the pope prisoner. This act marked the end of a process during which the papacy lost its iron grip on the governments of Western Europe. The judgment, the cleansing of the heavenly sanctuary, began shortly after this. Daniel 8:14 reveals the year when this judgment commenced. The 2,300 days (representing years) began in 457 B.C. and ended in A.D. 1844. In that year the work began of cleansing the heavenly sanctuary of the record of pardoned sin. God's living people are being examined to determine who has received the character of Christ.

THE TIME OF THE JUDGMENT.

What event mentioned in Daniel 8 is parallel to the pre-advent judgment of Daniel 7:9-14? Dan. 8:14. When did both the 70 weeks and the 2,300 days begin? Dan. 9:24, 25.

The cleansing of the sanctuary was to begin after 2,300 days (Dan. 8:14). Note these facts:

1. The phrase translated "days" means a 24-hour period. The Hebrew phrase is *ereb boqer*. It means literally "evening-morning." A form of this phrase is used some 22 times in the Hebrew Old Testament. When a 24-hour period is intended the phrase is always "evening-morning." (See Gen. 1:5, 8, 13, 19, 23, 31; Ex. 27:20, 21.) When the offering of the morning and evening sacrifice or the offering of incense is referred to, the phrase is always "morning-evening." (See 1 Chron. 16:40; 2 Chron. 2:4.) In Daniel 8:14, 26 the phrase is evening-morning, a 24-hour period. Daniel 8:14 is not speaking of 2,300 morning and evening sacrifices of the sanctuary; or 1,150 days. The reference is to 2,300 24-hour days.

2. The 2,300 days of Daniel 8:14 are symbolic of 2,300 years. The prophet was told that the work of the little horn power would continue till the end of time. (See Dan. 8:17, 19, 25, 26.) But 2,300 literal days would not reach to the end of time. They must refer to a period of centuries, not just a period of 6 years and 4 months. (See the day-for-a-year principle in Eze. 4:6; Num. 14:34.)

3. The "seventy weeks" (Hebrew: "seventy sevens") were to be "cut off" (Hebrew: *chathak*) from the beginning of the 2,300 days. These "seventy sevens" must refer to 490 years, because they were to reach down to the time of the Messiah. You cannot have 490 years cut off from 2,300 literal days. Therefore, the 2,300 days are a prophetic symbol of 2,300 years.

4. Both the 70 weeks and the 2,300 days began with "the going forth of the commandment to restore and to build Jerusalem" (Dan. 9:25). Ezra 6:14 indicates that God's commandment for the rebuilding of Jerusalem, the restoration of the temple and its services, and the re-establishment of the Jewish state was put into effect by the decrees of three Persian monarchs: Cyrus, Darius, and Artaxerxes. The decree of Artaxerxes I Longimanus was put into operation in the autumn of 457 B.C. (See S. H. Horn and L. H. Wood, *The Chronology of Ezra 7*, Review and Herald, 1953, 1970). And 2,300 years after the autumn of 457 B.C. brings us to the autumn of 1844, when the pre-advent judgment began.

What is the nature of the pre-advent judgment? What kinds of decision does it make? Matt. 22:11-14.

1. It takes place in heaven (Dan. 7:9).

2. It involves a court session in which books of record are examined (Dan. 7:9, 10). This is why we call it an "investigative judgment." (On the heavenly books of record, see the book of life [Luke 10:20; Phil. 4:3; Heb. 12:23; Rev. 20:12], the record of sins [Eccl. 12:14; Matt. 12:36, 37; Jer. 2:22; Rev. 20:12; 22:12], and the book of remembrance [Mal. 3:16, 17].)

3. The "Son of man" is the defense attorney in this judgment (Dan. 7:13). The title "Son of man" was Jesus' favorite name for Himself. (See Matt. 8:20.) Daniel 7:13 is not describing the second coming of Christ. The Son of man comes to the Ancient of Days (the Father), who is seated upon His throne before the heavenly court (verse 9). (See Ellen G. White, *The Great Controversy*, p. 424.)

4. Christ receives His kingdom in this judgment (Dan. 7:14). At the conclusion of the judgment, all those whose names have been retained in the book of life are delivered and saved eternally (Dan. 12:1). Those who once had their names in the book of life, but who did not retain their born-again experience, have had their names taken out of the book of life (Rev. 3:5). Salvation depends on maintaining our relationship with Jesus. (See Matt. 24:13.)

Judgment of the dead is followed by judgment of the living: Revelation 6:9-11 presents the dead martyrs as symbolic of all those who died believing. Metaphorically their blood is crying out to the Lord from the ground, "How long before thou wilt judge and avenge our blood?" (verse 10, RSV). The next verse indicates that they are vindicated and told to "rest a little longer." The judgment that vindicates them takes place a short time before Jesus' second advent. Verse 11 translates literally from the Greek: "And to each of them was given a white robe, and it was said to them that they should rest a little longer, until their fellow servants and their brethren who are *about to be killed* as they were *might be made complete*." The living believers are to be "made complete" in Christ during the pre-advent judgment. Then Christ will come and raise the righteous dead.

Revelation 7:1-3 speaks of the sealing of the living believers during the pre-advent judgment. When they are sealed, the latter part of Revelation 6:11 is fulfilled, and God's living people are ready to meet Jesus.

FURTHER STUDY: Read as much as you can from Ellen G. White's *The Great Controversy*, chapters 23, 24, and 28.

What will be the spiritual condition of God's people who are sealed during the pre-advent judgment? Revelation 14:1-5 expands on the meaning of the end-time sealing referred to in Revelation 7:1-3. The reception of the seal of God during the pre-advent judgment involves "his name and his Father's name written on their foreheads" (verse 1, RSV). The names of Christ and the Father are symbolic of their character. We are to receive the character of Christ by the indwelling of the Holy Spirit. (Compare Rom. 8:9, 10.) We will then be made permanently "complete in Christ" (Rev. 6:11). Then Revelation 14:5 will be fulfilled: "And in their mouth no lie was found, for they are spotless" (RSV). (Compare Rev. 19:2, 7, 8.)

None need fear the investigative judgment. Fellowship with Christ is the key to security. There is to be an unbroken union between our Lord and ourselves. As we look to Christ and His sacrifice, allowing His Holy Spirit to dwell in our hearts, we will have victory over Satan's power, will receive the seal of God, and will be ready to present Christ's last appeal to a lost world. Revelation 18:1-5 describes the last message presented worldwide by those filled with the glory of Christ's character. Then probation will close and Jesus will come (Rev. 22:11, 12).

DISCUSSION QUESTIONS:

1. **Do you believe that during the pre-advent judgment Jesus is able to give His living believers total victory over sin? If so, how? How has He always given His people victory over sin? (See 1 Peter 1:15, 16; 1 John 5:1-5.)**

2. **Even though Christ's believing people have victory over sin, do they retain their fallen natures until He comes the second time? (See 1 Cor. 15:49-54; Phil. 3:20, 21.)**

3. **When are the sins of Christian believers forgiven, at the moment of belief and confession or not until their cases are examined in the pre-advent judgment? (See 1 John 1:9; compare Lev. 4 and 16.)**

SUMMARY: Christ's sacrifice on the cross was followed by centuries of mediatorial ministry in the heavenly sanctuary. Although the ministry of forgiveness has continued since 1844, in that year the pre-advent, investigative judgment began. In this judgment the heavenly sanctuary is cleansed of the record of pardoned sin, and God's living people are spiritually purified as a preparation to meet their returning Lord.

Lesson 24

The Second Coming

OUR BLESSED HOPE. From the earliest days of our existence as a people, Seventh-day Adventists have shared enthusiastically the "blessed hope" in the second coming of Christ (Titus 2:13). As half of our denominational name indicates, we expect a literal second coming. Not only will Christ return but He will return soon, although He has not revealed the specific time for this event.

No one but God knows the exact time of the second coming (Matt. 24:36), yet by studying the prophecies and signs it is possible to know that "it is near, even at the doors" (Matt. 24:33). The second coming will bring the nations of the present age to an end. It will establish God's everlasting kingdom, the last of the kingdoms predicted in such lines of prophecy as Daniel 2. Christ's people will dwell forever with their eternal King.

KEY THOUGHT: The second coming of Christ will be literal, personal, visible, and worldwide. The almost complete fulfillment of most of the signs of Christ's return indicates that Christ's coming is near. Because the exact time of that event has not been revealed, we are exhorted to be ready at all times.

"The grace of God that bringeth salvation hath appeared to all men, teaching us that, denying ungodliness and worldly lusts, we should live soberly, righteously, and godly, in this present world; looking for that blessed hope, and the glorious appearing of the great God and our Saviour Jesus Christ" (Titus 2:11-13).

In recent years bumper stickers on some cars in the United States have raised the question, "Guess Who's Coming Again?" People in this country are talking about the end of the world and the second coming of Jesus to a degree not seen since the great Advent movement of the 1840s.

What is there about the promise that Jesus made in John 14:1-3 that has inspired His followers through the ages to look forward so enthusiastically to His return?

Facing the final crisis of His life on earth and ultimate separation from His disciples, Christ gave this glorious promise for the encouragement of His followers throughout the ages. It is one of the 318 times that His second coming is mentioned in the New Testament. One of the greatest assurances that we have of Christ's return comes from the way He fulfilled the prophecies of His first coming. John, the beloved disciple who reports Jesus' promise, also heard Jesus' last recorded promise to return, "Surely I come quickly," and responded enthusiastically, "Even so, come, Lord Jesus" (Rev. 22:20).

Indicate how the Old Testament contributes to our understanding of the second coming of Christ:

Job 19:25-27 _____

Ps. 50:3-5 _____

Dan. 2:44, 45 _____

True Christians live for the fulfillment of these prophecies. If they die before Jesus comes, they do so with this hope in their hearts. Why? Because true Christians love Jesus more than anyone else and long to be with Him.

If you hear that a loved one whom you have not seen for some time is coming soon to see you, how do you feel? What kind of information would you want to know about the impending visit? Most likely you would want to know why, when, and how the person was coming. You would also want to know how best to prepare for his or her arrival. This lesson seeks to answer these kinds of question about Jesus' return.

WHY WILL HE COME?

The reason for Jesus' second coming is that He loves His human brothers and sisters and wants them to be with Him. "I go to prepare a place for you," He told the first disciples. "And if I go and prepare a place for you, I will come again, and receive you unto myself; that where I am, there ye may be also" (John 14:2, 3). Jesus will take His beloved—including those who have died and are resurrected when He comes—to heaven with Him. (See 1 Thess. 4:16, 17.)

What all-inclusive reason for Christ's second coming is mentioned in Hebrews 9:28?

Here is the one text in the Bible that links the term *second* with Christ's return. Although many today are pessimistic about the future, Christ will come soon to make everything that is wrong right again.

Victory over the grave depends on the return of Jesus. Three important concepts can be found in 1 Corinthians 15:19-23. First, Paul holds out hope for all who accept Christ. That hope reaches beyond this life to include the life the righteous will receive on the resurrection day. Second, Paul argues that if there is no second coming of Christ, then there can be no resurrection of the dead. In that case our belief, hope, and trust in Christ would be quite futile. Third, Paul emphasizes the fact that the resurrection definitely takes place at Christ's coming.

What distinction is made in 1 Corinthians 15:51-54 between what happens to the righteous dead and the righteous living at Christ's return?

Notice that, whether righteous people are dead or living when Christ returns, the glorious gift of immortality is bestowed; never again are they to be haunted by the fear of death. Death will have lost its sting. The grave will have been robbed of the victory it has claimed.

What additional reason does John give for the second coming of Christ (Rev. 22:12)? How does this affect the way you view the judgment? What are the benefits of the judgment to the righteous on earth and to the universe as a whole?

WHEN WILL HE COME?

There are many lines of prophecy in the Scriptures, particularly in the books of Daniel and Revelation, that indicate Jesus will return soon. But here we will concentrate on Christ's own predictions about His second coming, predictions made during His ministry on earth.

What did Jesus say to the disciples as they left the temple that triggered their interest in the question of when these things would take place? Matt. 24:1-3.

In the prophecy that follows, Jesus answers both phases of the disciples' question. Thus the prophecy has a double application—first to the events that surrounded the destruction of Jerusalem in A.D. 70, and next to the time of His second coming. In verses 4-14 we find predictions that apply to both events. Verses 15-20 seem to find their primary fulfillment in the destruction of Jerusalem, although there is a parallel in our day. Jesus' description of the events that were to follow the destruction of Jerusalem as outlined in verses 21, 22 was fulfilled during the period from the time of that destruction through the middle of the eighteenth century.

The period of great tribulation was to be followed by a series of spectacular signs. (See verse 29.) Adventists generally are aware of the fulfillment of the signs in the sun, moon, and stars in 1780 and 1833. But what does Jesus' prophecy mean when it states that the "powers of the heavens shall be shaken"?

We have been given this insight: "I saw that when the Lord said 'heaven,' in giving the signs recorded by Matthew, Mark, and Luke, He meant heaven, and when He said 'earth' He meant earth. The powers of heaven are the sun, moon, and stars. They rule in the heavens. The powers of earth are those that rule on the earth. The powers of heaven will be shaken at the voice of God. Then the sun, moon, and stars will be moved out of their places. They will not pass away, but be shaken by the voice of God. . . . I saw that the powers of earth are now being shaken and that events come in order. War, and rumors of war, sword, famine, and pestilence are first to shake the powers of earth, then the voice of God will shake the sun, moon, and stars, and this earth also."—Ellen G. White, *Early Writings*, p. 41.

Notice what Luke adds to the prophetic outline that is not found in Matthew 24. Luke 21:25, 26.

Besides watching carefully the signs of Jesus' coming, we are to learn all that we can about the manner of His coming. The reason for this is that counterfeit "christs" will appear in the last days who will "deceive many" (Matt. 24:5).

What assurance do we have that Christ's coming will be literal, personal, and visible? Acts 1:11.

His second coming is not to be confused with the spiritual presence of Christ with believers since His ascension, with the descent of the Holy Spirit as Christ's representative, or with death.

Neither should we be confused by those who expect a "secret rapture." They believe that the parable of Christ's coming like a thief in the night points to a secret rapture. Hal Lindsey, author of the bestseller *The Late Great Planet Earth*, calls it "Project Disappearance." The idea is that Christians will be "caught up to meet the Lord in the air" suddenly—from whatever they are doing—such as: driving, piloting planes, teaching, and performing surgery. Imagine the colossal confusion that would result if people engaged in these types of activity suddenly disappeared!

How do we know from our study of the Bible that Christ will not come in the kind of "secret rapture" that many expect today? Here are some key texts to consider:

Matt. 24:26, 27, 30 _____

1 Thess. 4:16 _____

Rev. 1:7 _____

"Adding to the picture of a universal awareness of Christ's return is the Biblical assertion that His coming will be made known by sound as well as sight [1 Thess. 4:16 quoted]. . . . The 'great sound of a trumpet' (Matt. 24:31) accompanies the gathering of His people. There is no secrecy here."—*Seventh-day Adventists Believe*, (Hagerstown, Maryland: Review and Herald Publishing Assoc., 1988), p. 336.

With so many false concepts about Christ's return being circulated, what can I do to keep from being deceived?

What two essential steps should we take in order to make sure that we are ready for Jesus to come? Luke 21:36.

1. _____

2. _____

What did Jesus mean when He challenged those who want to be ready for His return to "watch"? He spelled out His meaning in detailed fashion in seven parables of preparedness found in Matthew 24:32–25:46.

Study carefully the chart below in order to understand better what it means to "watch" and to become aware of the attitudes that should characterize those longing for Christ's return:

Parables of Preparedness	Meaning of "Watch"	Attitude
24:32-35—Fig tree	Nearness	Awareness
24:36-42—As in the days of Noah	Unexpectedness	Watchfulness, concern
24:43, 44—Thief in the night	Readiness	Being on guard
24:45-51—Two types of servant	Responsibility	Faithfulness
25:1-13—Ten Virgins	Spiritual responsibility	Consecration, dedication
25:14-30—Talents	Diligence, accountability	Zeal, loving anxiety to share
25:31-46—Sheep and goats	Love	As Christ loved

What will those looking forward to Christ's soon return do to demonstrate that they belong to Him and wish to be with Him? 1 John 3:2, 3.

While we wait for Christ's return we must do what we can to make the world a better place, always keeping in mind that the ultimate goal is to prepare ourselves and others for the new world soon to come.

What changes in your lifestyle do you need to make in order to be ready to meet Jesus when He returns?

FURTHER STUDY:

What are some of the other happy consequences of the judgment and Christ's return?

Dan. 7:22 _____

2 Tim. 4:8 _____

Rev. 2:7 _____

Rev. 3:21 _____

Rev. 21:4 _____

Why does God not want us to know the exact day and hour of Christ's return? (See Matt. 24:36.)

Even though we may not know the exact day and hour, what can we know in regard to the time when Christ will return? Matt. 24:32, 33.

DISCUSSION QUESTIONS:

1. **How do you think you can present the second coming of Christ in an eager, exciting way, letting others see that you are looking forward to this great day?**

2. **As you await the coming of Christ, what part in your daily program do you give for Bible study, prayer, and witnessing as a means of drawing closer to the One you expect to meet soon? Are you able to look back on each day's activities and know that this day has been a steppingstone in preparation for Christ's return?**

SUMMARY: Our blessed hope is the literal, visible, audible, and personal second coming of Christ. The signs of His coming, apparent in a special way in these last remnants of time, thrill those who eagerly, expectantly await His return, motivating them to do their part in finishing God's work on earth. They invite the Holy Spirit to work in and through them in order that they may be prepared to go home to heaven with Christ when He comes and not be destroyed with those who are not ready for His return.

Lesson 25

Death and Resurrection

IS THERE LIFE AFTER DEATH? Newspapers often have stories and pictures of people who allegedly experienced life after being pronounced clinically dead. The concept of life after death is also vividly portrayed in some television programs.

In the early Christian centuries, Greek philosophical teaching of the immortality of the soul became largely accepted by Christians. Today many organizations and movements, some Christian and some non-Christian, attempt to give credence to the immortal-soul concept. The New Age movement is deeply committed to this teaching.

What happens when a person dies? Does his or her soul go to heaven or hell, or does it stay in the grave? Does the dead person know what is happening on earth? Can he or she, as many people believe, communicate with living loved ones? Will the circumstances of the dead ever change, or is death the end of it all?

KEY THOUGHT. The Bible teaches that death, the result of sin, is an unconscious state for all people. At the second coming of Christ the resurrected righteous and the living righteous will be given immortality and taken to heaven. The resurrection of the unrighteous will take place a thousand years later.

"For since by man came death, by man came also the resurrection of the dead. For as in Adam all die, even so in Christ shall all be made alive" (1 Corinthians 15:21, 22).

WHAT DID JESUS AND BIBLE PROPHETS TEACH ABOUT DEATH?

How did Christ's greatest miracle, the raising of Lazarus, reveal the state of man in death? What did Jesus call death? John 11:6, 7, 11-14.

Compare the following Bible passages with Jesus' teaching on the state of the dead: Job 14:10-12; Dan. 12:2; Matt. 27:52.

Never did Jesus or the Bible writers suggest that part of a person sleeps at death while another part goes on living in a conscious state. When the Bible writers faced death they did not expect to be conscious living beings again until God restores their existence at the second coming of Christ.

What do the following passages teach about how much knowledge the dead have? Eccl. 9:5, 6, 10; Job 14:21; Ps. 6:5; 115:17.

The Bible teaches that the dead are sleeping, without any awareness of events on earth or in heaven. They do not praise God, because they cannot. If the good were in heaven immediately after death, wouldn't they praise the Lord?

The parable of the rich man and Lazarus (Luke 16:19-31) teaches the danger of selfishness. It indicates that there is no second chance after death. It offers no support for the doctrine of the immortality of the soul. If the parable is interpreted literally, it becomes an absurdity. For example, the beggar went to "Abraham's bosom." Obviously that is a symbol. The rich man in hell spoke of Lazarus' finger and his own tongue. In this parable the dead have bodies. But immortal-soul advocates believe that the souls of the dead are disembodied. The rich man wanted Lazarus to go to his living brothers and warn them. This could happen only if "one rose from the dead" (Luke 16:31), not by dead souls communicating with the living.

Jesus was using a popular fable as a sermon illustration. He was not teaching life immediately after death, or the doctrine of the immortality of the soul. The first-century Jewish historian Josephus tells much the same fable in other words. (See "An Extract Out of Josephus' Discourse to the Greeks Concerning Hades" in *Josephus—Complete Works*, translated by William Whiston [Grand Rapids, Mich.: Kregel, 1960], pp. 637, 638).

The Bible explains where the dead are not, as well as where they are.

Where did David not go when he died, despite the fact that he was a righteous man whose sins had been forgiven? Acts 2:29, 34.

In his great sermon on the Day of Pentecost, the apostle Peter explained that David's statement in Psalm 16 was a reference to the Messiah, not to David himself (Acts 2:24-33). Peter pointed out that David was dead and buried, and his grave was there for everyone to see. Christ rose from the dead and ascended to heaven, but David remained in the grave, where his body experienced corruption. David was a righteous man, but he did not go to heaven when he died.

The Bible nowhere teaches that believers in Christ go to heaven when they die.

According to Isaiah, where are the dead? Isa. 26:19.

Where would Job wait for the change that only God can bring to the dead? Job 14:14; 17:13-16.

Where are the dead? Job and Isaiah answer very positively. The dead are in the dust of the earth, resting in their graves, waiting for the great change that Jesus promised would come at the end of time.

Believers in Christ need not fear death. Because it is a state of unconsciousness, they will rest peacefully until the call of the Lifegiver. If the dead were in heaven seeing the struggles of their loved ones on earth, how could they ever be happy? If they were in hell, suffering for long periods of time until the second coming of the Lord, it would be difficult to understand how a God of love could bring such protracted suffering. It would seem that such punishment would be excessive even for the most wicked sinner.

How does the Bible teaching that death is a state of complete unconsciousness change our understanding of hell? What does the biblical teaching of death as a sleep do for the idea of purgatory? How does the Bible position regarding the dead improve our concept of the nature of God?

WHAT IS A HUMAN "SPIRIT"?

Many think the "spirit" of an individual goes on living either in heaven or hell. Does the Bible teach this view?

What were the component parts of humans given by God at Creation? Gen. 2:7. What happens to these components when a person dies? Ps. 146:3, 4; Eccl. 12:7.

The breath of life (spirit) given to humans at Creation was the life principle, or life force, that gave life to the body and existence to the individual. When a person dies the creation process is reversed. The breath of life (spirit) goes back to God, and the body goes back to the dust of the earth. The words "breath" (Ps. 146:4) and "spirit" (Eccl. 12:7) are a translation of the Hebrew word *ruach*. The Greek equivalent used in the New Testament is *pneuma*. These words have a number of meanings:
   1. Breath of the mouth (Dan. 10:17; 2 Thess. 2:8).
   2. Breath of air, wind, soft breeze (Ex. 14:21; John 3:8).
   3. The Spirit of God (Gen. 1:2; John 14:17).
   4. An evil spirit (1 Sam. 16:23; Luke 11:24).
   5. The principle that gives life to the body (Gen. 6:17; Luke 8:55).
   6. The emotions, intellectual functions, and attitudes of the will (Gen. 41:8; 2 Cor. 2:13).

Never in Scripture is the "spirit" of a human said to survive the death of the body as an immortal, conscious entity. In Ecclesiastes 3:19-21 the "spirit" is the life force implanted by God at Creation and shared by every living thing, whether human or animal. (Compare Gen. 7:15, 21, 22.)

Some interpreters of the Bible misuse Ecclesiastes 12:7, attempting to prove that the immortal spirits of good people go to heaven when they die. If the *spirit* in this verse is a person's immortal soul, then the souls of *all* people, good and bad, must go to heaven when they die. But no one believes that the spirits of evil persons ascend to heaven at death. The text simply teaches that the *life principle*, the spirit, given by God to all people, is taken back by God when they die. The immortality of the soul is not even implied.

Both Old and New Testaments sometimes use the word *spirit* to refer to the mind of humans, their capacity to reason, as well as their ability to feel and choose. (See Dan. 2:1; 5:12; Matt. 26:41; Rom. 1:9.) Such intellectual and emotional faculties never survive the death of the body.

WHAT IS A "SOUL"? IS IT IMMORTAL?

Immortality is the capacity to never die. Did God create man with an immortal soul? Genesis 2:7 says that the body + the breath of life = "a living soul." That implies that if the breath of life were withdrawn, a person would be a dead soul. If souls can die, they are not immortal.

What do the following passages teach regarding the soul? Eze. 18:4; Rev. 16:3; Matt. 10:28.

The Hebrew word for soul used in the Old Testament is *nephesh*. The Greek equivalent used in the New Testament is *psuche*. In Numbers 6:6 the Hebrew word for "soul" is translated "body" (KJV). The same word is translated as "creature" in Genesis 1:20, 21, 30; 2:19; 9:10, 12, 15, 16 (KJV). All of these passages speak of animals as souls. God made animals living souls just as He made man a living soul. Like humans, when the animals die, they are dead souls.

Compare man's life with God's. Who only has immortality? 1 Tim. 6:15, 16.

Because God "only hath immortality," human souls are not immortal. The human soul has two parts: the body and the breath. Without the one the other cannot exist. The death of the body is the death of the soul.

Kittel's *Theological Dictionary of the New Testament* comments on the Hebrew word for "soul" (*nephesh*): The soul "has no existence apart from the body. Hence the best translation in many instances is 'person' comprised in corporeal reality. . . . Hence *nephesh* [soul] can denote what is most individual in human nature, namely the ego, and it can become a synonym for the personal pronoun, Gn. 27:25."—Volume IX, p. 620.

The New Testament Greek word for soul (*psuche*) has meanings similar to those of the Old Testament word. It is often best translated by "life." A human life is a "soul." (See Mark 3:4; 8:35 where the KJV and RSV translate the Greek word for "soul" as "life.")

Nowhere in the Scriptures is the soul spoken of as a disembodied immortal entity in heaven or hell. The word *soul* can mean the total personality or part of it. When the body dies, so do the other faculties of the soul.

WILL THE DEAD LIVE AGAIN?

What do the following passages teach regarding the resurrection of the dead?

John 5:28, 29 _____

Acts 24:15 _____

1 Cor. 15:16-22, 51-54 _____

2 Cor. 4:14 _____

1 Thess. 4:13-18 _____

The first two passages above indicate there are two resurrections: (1) "the resurrection of life," which is the resurrection of the "just," (2) "the resurrection of damnation," which is the resurrection of the "unjust." The first resurrection takes place at the second coming of Jesus. This is when all of Christ's faithful people, those who are raised from the dead and those who are translated without seeing death, are given immortality. All of these faithful ones are taken to heaven with perfect bodies and minds. (See John 14:1-3; Rev. 7:13-17; Ellen G. White, *The Great Controversy*, pp. 644, 645.)

The second resurrection (in which those are raised who died unbelieving) takes place 1,000 years later. (See Rev. 20:5, first part, 7-9.) The lost are never given immortality. They are consumed in the fires of the last great day. They do not live on to suffer for eternity.

Note the teaching of the following passages:

Mal. 4:1, 3 _____

Ps. 37:10, 20 _____

Ps. 68:1, 2 _____

These texts teach that the wicked will be completely destroyed. The Bible passages that use the phrase "for ever and ever" (Rev. 14:11; 20:10) refer to the suffering of the wicked for as long as their particular nature allows. The Greek words may refer to a period of limited duration. In the case of the wicked, the limit is determined by their mortality. They are destroyed by fire at the end of the millennium.

FURTHER STUDY: On the meaning of "everlasting destruction" (2 Thess. 1:9) compare: Jude 7; 2 Pet. 2:6; Jer. 17:27; 2 Chron. 36:19, 21. On the meaning of "forever" (Rev. 14:11; 20:10) compare: Jonah 2:6; 1:17; Matt. 12:40; 2 Kings 5:27; Ex. 12:24. On the danger of the immortal-soul doctrine read Ellen G. White, *The Great Controversy*, pp. 531-562.

DISCUSSION QUESTIONS:

1. Your neighbor, who does not believe in Christ, becomes terminally ill. How would you explain to him or her that there is hope beyond the grave? What part of the Bible teaching would you especially emphasize?

2. What is the next thing faithful believers in Christ know after death, even if they have been in the grave for centuries? Why, then, is the Bible teaching of death as a sleep not discomforting by contrast with the view that believers go to heaven immediately after death?

3. What are the special dangers today in believing the unbiblical doctrine of the immortality of the soul?

4. How does the Bible teaching on the state of the dead destroy the notion of the reincarnation of the soul? How does it destroy the idea that the spirits of the dead can communicate with their living loved ones?

5. Why should you not fear death? Under what circumstances should anyone be afraid to die?

SUMMARY: The Bible teaches that, because of Calvary, death is a temporary sleep for all human beings. There is no immortal part of man that lives on after the death of the body. At the second coming of Jesus, the righteous dead are raised and, along with their living brethren, given immortality. At the end of the 1,000 years, the wicked are raised, punished according to their works, and put to sleep for eternity.

Lesson 26

The Millennium

ADVENTISTS ARE PREMILLENNIALISTS. Adventists believe that Christ's second advent occurs before the millennium and that God raised up the Seventh-day Adventist Church for the special purpose of proclaiming the everlasting gospel to the world in the setting of the three angels' messages. At the heart of these messages is the announcement that the "hour of his judgment is come" (Rev. 14:7). The judgment began in 1844 as Christ began His Most Holy–apartment ministry in the heavenly sanctuary. As mentioned in the lesson that dealt with the Bible teaching on the judgment, there are four phases. This lesson shows how these four phases of the judgment fit into the framework of the millennium of Revelation 20.

KEY THOUGHT. The millennium is the thousand-year period that takes place after the second coming of Jesus. During this time the earth will be utterly desolate, occupied only by Satan and his angels. At its close Christ with His saints and the Holy City will descend from heaven to earth. The unrighteous dead will be resurrected, and with Satan and his angels will be destroyed by fire from God. The universe will be freed of sin forever.

"Nevertheless we, according to his promise, look for new heavens and a new earth, wherein dwelleth righteousness" (2 Peter 3:13).

THE MILLENNIUM—THE PERIOD BETWEEN TWO RESURRECTIONS.

The book of Revelation describes a period of 1,000 years known to Bible students as "the millennium." The term *millennium* is not in the Bible, but is derived from two Latin words— *mille*, meaning "1,000," and *annum*, meaning "year." In discussions of the prophecies, Bible students use the term to refer exclusively to the 1,000-year period set forth in Revelation 20. The millennium begins with a resurrection and ends with a resurrection.

What does the Bible call the resurrection that begins the 1,000-year period? Rev. 20:6.

This resurrection is limited to the righteous dead, those who are "blessed and holy."

When are the rest of the dead resurrected? Rev. 20:5.

The righteous who are raised in the first resurrection come forth with perfect, immortal bodies. The wicked are raised in the second resurrection with the same kind of weak mortal bodies they had when they died.

Notice how Jesus distinguished between the two resurrections mentioned in John 5:28, 29. He called the first the "resurrection of life" and the second the "resurrection of condemnation" (NRSV). Also notice in the bar at the top of the chart how the events that take place at the time of the first resurrection *precede* the 1,000 years and those that take place at the time of the second resurrection *follow* the 1,000 years.

The Bible teaches that the coming of Christ takes place before the millennium. This is called premillennialism. Another view held by some Christians is known as postmillennialism. Those holding this position believe that a future golden age of blessedness will take place before Christ comes the second time. But the Bible teaches that the world will suffer conflict and trouble before Jesus comes. Those taking a postmillennialist position are not in agreement with the Scriptures on this point.

Can you think of any reason why the position we take on the placement of the millennium might make a difference in our Christian experience? Does it make a difference in our anticipation and preparedness for the second coming?

Six events precede the millennium.

1. The return of Jesus. This is the climax of what are known as the "last days." (See Rev. 19:11-16.)

2. The righteous dead raised. Revelation 20:4 describes the righteous in heaven. How did they get there? Revelation 20:6 explains. Note how the Bible connects the resurrection of the righteous with the second coming of Christ (1 Thess. 4:15-17).

3. Satan bound. Revelation 20:1-3 describes Satan being bound at the beginning of the 1,000 years. What does it mean for Satan to be bound? Ever since he first tempted Adam and Eve in the Garden of Eden, Satan has occupied himself with trying to deceive people and lead them into sin. But with the righteous in heaven and the wicked in their graves, he will have nothing to do. The Bible pictures him as being bound with a chain (Rev. 20:1, 2). The chain is symbolic, not literal. The translation of the righteous and the death of the wicked are links in the chain that will bind Satan. He will be isolated on this desolated earth without anyone to tempt.

4. Living saints caught up. First Thessalonians 4:16, 17 indicates that those gathered will include both the righteous who are living when Jesus comes and the righteous who are resurrected at His coming. The righteous do not remain on the earth. Before Jesus went away He gave the wonderful promise: "I will come again, and receive you unto myself; that where I am, there ye may be also" (John 14:2, 3). That place is heaven. The saints will live and reign there with Christ during the thousand years (Rev. 20:4-6).

5. The wicked slain. Where will the wicked be during the millennium? Rev. 20:5.

6. The earth desolated. Jeremiah 4:23-27 describes the desolation of Judah during the captivity in terms that indicate there would be a broader, more significant application at the end of time. It can be applied to the condition of this earth after Jesus has taken the saints to heaven. Note the universal extent of the desolation.

How do these predicted events affect your determination to serve Christ?

What is the significance of the place where Revelation 15:2-4 pictures those standing who have gained the victory over the beast and its image and have been taken to heaven at the second coming? What are they doing?

"They are no longer feeble, afflicted, scattered, and oppressed. Henceforth they are to be ever with the Lord. They stand before the throne clad in richer robes than the most honored of the earth have ever worn. They are crowned with diadems more glorious than were ever placed upon the brow of earthly monarchs. The days of pain and weeping are forever ended. The King of glory has wiped the tears from all faces; every cause of grief has been removed. Amid the waving of palm branches they pour forth a song of praise, clear, sweet, and harmonious; every voice takes up the strain, until the anthem swells through the vaults of heaven: 'Salvation to our God which sitteth upon the throne, and unto the Lamb.' "—Ellen G. White, *The Great Controversy*, p. 650.

Analyze what the following texts say about the judgment of the wicked that takes place in heaven during the millennium:

1 Cor. 4:5 _____

1 Cor. 6:2, 3 _____

Rev. 20:4, 6 _____

"In union with Christ they judge the wicked, comparing their acts with the statute book, the Bible, and deciding every case according to the deeds done in the body. Then the portion which the wicked must suffer is meted out, according to their works; and it is recorded against their names in the book of death."—Ellen G. White, *The Great Controversy*, p. 661. This phase of judgment is part of God's plan for demonstrating to the universe that He is both just and merciful. Before He destroys sin and sinners, He must be sure that the entire universe agrees with His decisions.

What do you think about whether there will be sorrow and tears in heaven during the examination of the records of those we have loved on earth? In what way will we come to better understand God's love for those who are lost?

WHAT TAKES PLACE ON EARTH DURING THE MILLENNIUM?

Revelation 20:5 states that the "rest of the dead" will not live again "until the thousand years were finished." At the second coming, the saints will be taken to heaven to reign with Christ during the thousand years while the wicked will have been destroyed by the brightness of His coming. This leaves the earth depopulated. Satan is bound by circumstances, for he now has no one to tempt.

What is meant by the "bottomless pit" (Rev. 20:1, 3)? This "bottomless pit" is our earth. At Christ's coming, through earthquakes, storms, and human violence, this earth will be reduced to chaos. (See Rev. 16:18-21; Isa. 6:11.)

How can Isaiah's portrayal of the destruction of Israel help us understand the conditions that will prevail on earth during the millennium?

Isa. 24:1—The earth is _____

Verse 3—The land will be utterly _____

and _____.

Verse 5—The earth is _____.

Verse 6—The curse has _____ the earth.

Because this prophecy originally was addressed to literal Israel and intended to describe the destruction of their land by their enemies, not everything in these verses can be applied to the millennium. But the destruction described is so universal that it cannot be limited to the destruction of Israel. It contains a broader description that is applicable to the destruction of the earth at Christ's second coming.

"For a thousand years, Satan will wander to and fro in the desolate earth to behold the results of his rebellion against the law of God. During this time his sufferings are intense. Since his fall his life of unceasing activity has banished reflection; but he is now deprived of his power and left to contemplate the part which he has acted since first he rebelled against the government of heaven, and to look forward with trembling and terror to the dreadful future when he must suffer for all the evil that he has done and be punished for the sins that he has caused to be committed."—Ellen G. White, *The Great Controversy*, p. 660.

EVENTS AT THE CLOSE OF THE MILLENNIUM.

Six events also mark the close of the millennium:

1. Christ, the saints, and the city descend. Revelation 20:9 speaks of the "camp of the saints," or the beloved city, being on earth at the end of the millennium. It came "down from God out of heaven" (Rev. 21:2). The New Jerusalem and its inhabitants, including God Himself, come to earth to dwell (Rev. 21:3). "Our little world, under the curse of sin the one dark blot in His [God's] glorious creation, will be honored above all other worlds in the universe of God. Here . . . the tabernacle of God shall be with men."—Ellen G. White, *The Desire of Ages*, p. 26.

2. The wicked dead raised. (See Rev. 20:5.) The wicked come to life at the end of the 1,000 years.

3. Satan loosed. (See Rev. 20:7, 8.) God and the saints return to earth, and the wicked dead are raised. Once again Satan has someone to deceive. Thus he is "loosed" for a little season.

4. The last judgment. The last phase of the judgment is the executive judgment of the wicked, when God will be able (because of the three phases now completed) to do away with sin and its effect forever. Notice how this awesome judgment is described in Revelation 20:9-15.

5. Satan and sinners destroyed. The fire God uses to destroy sin and sinners does not burn eternally—its *consequences* are eternal. Three phrases in Malachi 4:1 demonstrate that the final judgment fire does not burn eternally: "Shall be *stubble*," "Shall burn them *up*," "Shall leave them neither *root* nor *branch*."

6. The earth cleansed and renewed. At the end of the millennium, Satan and those who have followed him in rebellion will be destroyed. (See Rev. 20:10.) The universe will be free from sin. And then God will re-create this earth as the eternal home of the saved. "And the years of eternity . . . will bring richer and still more glorious revelations of God and Christ. As knowledge is progressive, so will love, reverence, and happiness increase. The more men learn of God, the greater will be their admiration of His character. As Jesus opens before them the riches of redemption and the amazing achievements in the great controversy with Satan, the hearts of the ransomed thrill with more fervent devotion."—Ellen G. White, *The Great Controversy*, p. 678.

FURTHER STUDY: On the restoration of God's people on this earth at the end of the millennium, read: Amos 9:11-15; Eze. 20:40-44; Jer. 33:7-16; Joel 3:14-21; Rev. 21:1-5.

DISCUSSION QUESTIONS:
1. **How does the presentation of the details that take place at the end of the millennium help those who believe in an eternally burning hell recognize the error of that teaching?**

2. **What does the millennium doctrine do for your sense of security?**

3. **How can you ensure that you will be with Christ and the saved during the millennium?**

SUMMARY: The time between the world's end and its re-creation as the new earth is called the millennium. During this thousand years the wicked dead know not anything, the righteous living are in heaven, and Satan and his angels are confined to this desolate planet. For the saved, the millennium will be a time of reflection, judgment, and investigation as to why the wicked were lost. It will lead to a validation of the love and justice of God. It also will be a time of reflection for Satan and his fallen angels. This period will end in an irrevocable eradication of sin and sinners. Planet Earth will be renewed and restored to its Edenic beauty and populated by those who have surrendered to Christ and maintained a close relationship with Him.

Lesson 27

The New Earth

WHAT WILL LIFE BE LIKE ON THE NEW EARTH? Many questions come to mind when we consider the condition of the saved in the earth made new. First is the question, When is the earth made new? The previous lesson emphasized that during the 1,000 years after Jesus' second coming the saved will be in heaven, while this earth will be in a state of desolation, inhabited only by Satan and his evil demons. How does God change that situation?

What will the saved be like spiritually and physically? It is difficult to imagine a world free from temptation, hatred, discrimination, and war, free from sickness, disease, and death. Is there any possibility that evil will reappear after God has recreated the earth? Will the saved have complete security without any fear that their world of glory and peace will be shattered by some new threat? How do we prepare to inhabit the earth made new?

KEY THOUGHT. On the earth made new God's people will dwell in perfect security and happiness. Immortal and incorruptible, they will have opportunity for an eternity of spiritual and intellectual development, with the loving Lord as their ever-present Sovereign.

"And I saw a new heaven and a new earth: for the first heaven and the first earth were passed away; and there was no more sea. And I John saw the holy city, new Jerusalem, coming down from God out of heaven, prepared as a bride adorned for her husband" (Revelation 21:1, 2).

When do Christ and the saved descend to this earth? Rev. 21:2; 20:7-9.

At the end of the millennium Satan will be released from his prison of isolation when the wicked dead are raised to life. Then he and his demons once again will have people to tempt. Christ with the saved will descend from heaven (Zech. 14:4, 5, 9) followed by the holy city, the New Jerusalem, which comes to rest on this earth. Satan will lead his hosts of lost to besiege the city with the plan of making an assault upon it. At that point their plan will be interrupted by Christ's appearing on the "great white throne" above the city. (See Rev. 20:11.) The final judgment will take place, and fire will come down from heaven, destroying the wicked and purifying the earth. (See Ellen G. White, *The Great Controversy*, pp. 664-673.)

What does God do immediately after the destruction of the lost? Rev. 21:1; 2 Peter 3:13, 14.

Before the wondering gaze of the redeemed from within the holy city, the deformed old world is converted into a paradise of unexcelled loveliness.

What did Isaiah write regarding God's intention to renew the earth? Isa. 65:17, 18, 21, 22; 66:22.

Isaiah described a renewed Israel (Isaiah 11, 33, 35, 65, 66), promised by God to His repentant people. These prophecies were conditional, dependent on Israel's return to God. Since Israel failed, Isaiah's prophecies about a new Israel were not fulfilled. These prophecies will be ultimately fulfilled in the new earth promised by God to spiritual Israel.

What a picture of permanence and security! No more building and someone else inhabiting, no more planting and someone else reaping, no more end of life. There will be no painful reminders of our former misery. The Lord's assurances and promises are certain to be fulfilled.

How does knowledge of the blessings in store for God's redeemed people affect your attitude toward life in the here and now?

What is the New Jerusalem called? How does John describe it? Rev. 21:9-26; compare 19:7, 8.

The New Jerusalem is called "the bride, the Lamb's wife" (Rev. 21:9). It is the home of Christ's faithful people who were "married" to Christ during their earthly sojourn. Both the people and the city are called the bride because the city is the eternal home of the real bride—those who before the Advent were judged worthy of eternal life.

The frequency of the number 12 in the description of the city indicates its perfect symmetry. It is a perfect home for a spiritually perfected people. The wall of jasper, the city itself of translucent gold, the foundations of precious stones, the gates of pearl, the massive size—all suggest to the mind the most beautiful architectural wonder the human mind could possibly conceive.

"Once a sister wrote to me and asked if I would not tell her something about the city of our God, further than we have in the Word. She asked me if I could not draw something of its plans. I wrote her that I would have to say to her, 'Put off thy shoes from off thy feet, for the place whereon thou standest is holy ground.' 'No,' said I, 'you cannot paint, you cannot picture, and the martyr tongue cannot begin to give any description of the glory of the future life; but I will tell you what you can do: you can "press toward the mark for the prize of the high calling of God in Christ Jesus." You can die to self; you can seek to grow up to the perfection of Christian character in Christ Jesus.' That is our work; but when men begin to meddle with God's Word, I want to tell them to take their hands off, for they do not know what they are doing."—Ellen G. White Comments, *SDA Bible Commentary*, vol. 7, p. 920.

Why is there no temple in the New Jerusalem? Rev. 21:22.

When the saved are translated to heaven at the second coming of Jesus, they are taken to God's temple. (See Rev. 7:15; compare 20:4.) This is the heavenly sanctuary spoken of in Hebrews 8:1, 2, in which the sin problem is finally disposed of during the millennium. After that there is no need of a temple. Sin has at last been excluded from the universe.

WHAT IS THE SPIRITUAL CONDITION OF THE SAVED?

When Jesus said, "My kingdom is not of this world" (John 18:36), He meant that His kingdom is spiritual, not temporal; not characterized by worldly power or human pride. His eternal kingdom on the earth-made-new will be primarily a spiritual realm in which holiness is perfectly manifested.

Who will dwell with the saved for eternity on the earth made new? Rev. 21:3.

Paul wrote of Christian experience on this earth as freedom in Christ. "Christ is all, and in all" (Col. 3:11). On the earth made new the redeemed will look up to Jesus as the only One who bridged the terrible gap created by sin. He will be their eternal fulfillment. Apart from Him there would be no meaningful everlasting life. Throughout eternity Christians will ever hunger and thirst for more of Jesus—more understanding of His human life and works, more communion with Him, more time witnessing with Him to unfallen worlds. They will ever seek to become more like Him.

Of what will the saved partake throughout eternity? Rev. 7:17; 21:6; 22:2, 17; compare John 4:14.

In the new earth, the river of life flows "out of the throne of God and of the Lamb" (Rev. 22:1), and runs parallel with the city's street. The tree of life forms an arch over the river, with roots on both sides (Rev. 22:2). Every month it will bear new fruit. Throughout eternity the saved will partake of the tree of life and the water of life. This symbolizes that their perpetual existence, both spiritually and physically, will be maintained by their constant union with Christ.

Isaiah's description of a renewed Israel includes specific days of worship. Which of these would you expect to be observed in the new earth? Isa. 66:23.

"So long as the heavens and the earth endure, the Sabbath will continue as a sign of the Creator's power. And when Eden shall bloom on earth again, God's holy rest day will be honored by all beneath the sun."—Ellen G. White, *The Desire of Ages*, p. 283.

WHAT PHYSICAL AND MATERIAL BLESSINGS ARE ENJOYED BY THE SAVED?

Several Bible authors describe God's intention for His redeemed:

Isa. 11:6-9 _____

Isa. 35:5-10 _____

Isa. 65:17-25 _____

1 Cor. 13:12 _____

Phil. 3:20, 21 _____

The new earth is a real place inhabited by real people with real emotions and feelings, who will experience the real life that God intended for our parents in Eden. The new earth is a place where we will know our friends and loved ones, and be known by them. We will perform real work with real hands and enjoy the results of our labor. It will not be the arduous labor of this fallen world, but the most satisfying and fulfilling work. There will be opportunity to pursue every noble ambition.

Isaiah 65:20 does not mean that sin and death will exist on the new earth. Isaiah's message initially was given to Israel as a nation. Israel could have enjoyed great blessings, if the people had followed the will of God. There would have been little infant mortality, little physical sickness. Because of Israel's failure, the promises to her have been inherited by the Christian church. (See Gal. 3:28, 29.) Now the secondary application of Isaiah's prophecy applies. Those features involving sin and death no longer have relevance. But the predictions concerning the "new heavens" and the "new earth" run parallel with those of John in the book of Revelation.

"The great controversy is ended. Sin and sinners are no more. The entire universe is clean. One pulse of harmony and gladness beats through the vast creation. From Him who created all, flow life and light and gladness, throughout the realms of illimitable space. From the minutest atom to the greatest world, all things, animate and inanimate, in their unshadowed beauty and perfect joy, declare that God is love."—Ellen G. White, *The Great Controversy*, p. 678.

What is Jesus' earnest desire for each of us? John 17:24.

What is the spiritual qualification for inhabiting the new earth? Rev. 14:3-5; 21:7, 8, 27.

Christ will accept as a subject for His kingdom the person who, by His grace, overcomes sin. Throughout the book of Revelation, emphasis is given to the blessings for the over-comer. (See Revelation 2 and 3.) Christ craves to give us the victory that He experienced. (See Rev. 3:21.) He offers all the necessary power to make us conquerors. (See Jude 24; 1 John 5:2-4.)

What assurances do we have of the presence of Christ and the Father in our hearts as the source of our spiritual power? John 14:18, 23; 17:23; Gal. 2:20.

You can be an overcomer because of your spiritual union with Christ. He wants to dwell within you by His Holy Spirit and live out His life through you. There are enormous material and physical blessings for the saved in the new earth. But the real issue confronting us today is spiritual. Christ is offering spiritual advantages: victory over all sin, and purity of heart and mind. (See 2 Cor. 7:1; 1 Peter 1:15, 16.) These blessings can be yours now and forever. The spiritual qualities that will characterize the saved are to be yours now, because Jesus offers Himself to you now. His righteousness is yours now (Rom. 8:9, 10). His presence in your heart is yours now.

Christ assures us that what we give up for Him is not for our best good to retain. What a thrill we will have in the new earth of being totally free from the demands of fallen natures and the attacks of the evil one! The apostle John assures us that "we shall be like him; for we shall see him as he is" (1 John 3:2). Ultimate spiritual liberty will be the experience of God's re-deemed people. In the truest sense, they will be free at last!

Are you at this time willing to surrender your life entirely to Christ so that He can prepare you for life in the land where there is no sin? Will you commit yourself to cooperating with Him daily as He molds your character?

FURTHER STUDY: Read Isaiah 65, 66, and *The Great Controversy*, pp. 674-678.

The following principle is important to remember: "We should not be so anxious to gain the reward as to do what is right, irrespective of all gain. Love to God and to our fellow men should be our motive."—Ellen G. White, *Christ's Object Lessons*, pp. 398, 399.

The great motivation is not the mansions in which we will live, the gardens we will plant, and the joy we will have free from pain, sickness, and death. Even though that is all good, the most powerful motivation is the eternal fellowship we will have with the One who, for the sake of our redemption, left the fellowship of heaven and risked failure and eternal loss.

DISCUSSION QUESTIONS:

1. What would you say to a person who does not believe there will be an afterlife as described in this lesson?

2. Because heaven and the new earth will involve perfect peace and harmony, what should be our earnest endeavor now in our homes, in our community, and in our relationship to those of other races and cultures?

3. Why do you think the unrighteous dead are raised again at the end of the millennium? Why are they not left in their graves to sleep on for eternity?

4. Try to describe in your own words what it will be like to have no propensity to sin and no temptation. What kind of person will you be?

SUMMARY: The Bible teaches that God will restore our world to its original state of perfection at the end of the millennium when the New Jerusalem will descend from heaven. After the earth has been purged of sin and its results, God's people will be spiritually, intellectually, and physically perfect in a paradise of Edenic loveliness. God will be their King throughout the ceaseless ages of eternity.